The Complete Story of Tishrei

בס"ד

SOLIHULL & DISTRICT CHEDER CLASSES

This Prize awarded to ......CLAIRE LEVERMORE.

of Class ..II......... *For* ....Excellence...............

....

Date: 17.7.83.

Signed........................ Signed ....
President

ב"ה

THE COMPLETE STORY OF TISHREI

NISSAN MINDEL

Merkos L'inyonei Chinuch
770 Eastern Parkway, Brooklyn, N.Y. 11213

Revised Edition,

First Edition, eight printings, 1956-1978.
Revised Edition, first printing 1982.

Merkos L'inyonei Chinuch, Inc.

770 Eastern Parkway
Brooklyn, N.Y. 11213

Library of Congress Card Number: 82-81722
ISBN: 0-8266-0316-5

CONTENTS

PREFACE

The most colorful month in the Jewish calendar is undoubtedly, the first, Tishrei. The special festivals celebrated during this month span the spectrum of Jewish experience, from the solemn days of Rosh Hashanah and Yom Kippur, to the festive rejoicing of Sukkot, Shemini Atzeret and Simchat Torah. Each festival is saturated with its own unique flavor, each with its Mitzvot, customs, laws and observances.

The purpose of this volume is to present a comprehensive, thorough and well-balanced documention of all the aspects of these festivals — historical, liturgical and practical, liberally interspersed with popular stories and parables which educate as well as entertain.

The author has endeavored to bring out the essential flavor, spiritual richness and inner meaning of each festival. It is hoped that this will enable the reader to better understand and appreciate these festivals, and thereby be inspired to a more meaningful observance.

The author has drawn on the rich original sources of the Torah, Talmud and Midrash, as well as Rabbinic and Chassidic writings.

THE COMPLETE STORY OF TISHREI is a companion to the popular COMPLETE FESTIVAL SERIES by the same author, published by Merkos L'inyonei Chinuch. The festivals covered in that volume are: Chanukkah, Purim, Passover and Shavuot. (They are available individually, or in one volume.) Combined, the two volumes cover all the festivals in the Jewish calendar, and offer excellent source material for both school and home.

The author wishes to record his gratitude to the Lubavitcher Rebbe, Rabbi Menachem M. Schneerson, שליט"א, renowned leader of world Jewry, for taking time to peruse the manuscript of the present volume, as also of the previous ones, and making many useful suggestions and critical observations regarding the material presented. A special message from the Rebbe שליט"א, is included in this volume.

Nissan Mindel

PREFACE TO REVISED EDITION

The success of the COMPLETE STORY OF TISHREI has been overwhelming, as evidenced from the eight reprints it has seen, and from the many languages it has been translated into. This newly revised edition includes new illustrations by Mordechai Dorfman.

Nissan Mindel
Long Beach, N.Y.
Nissan, 5742

THE NEW YEAR IS COMING

ON THE THRESHOLD OF THE NEW YEAR

Forty Days of Grace

ROSH HASHANAH, the New Year, does not find the Jew unprepared. Already on Rosh Chodesh Elul, a whole month in advance, the arrival of Rosh Hashanah is heralded by the call of the Shofar, which is sounded at the conclusion of the Morning Services in the synagogue, and repeated every weekday until the day before Rosh Hashanah.

This custom of sounding the Shofar since the first day of Elul, although not a command in the Torah, dates back, our Sages say, to the days of Moses. On the first day of Elul Moses went up on Mount Sinai to spend there forty days and forty nights for the third time. He spent the first forty days on Sinai when he went up on the seventh day of Sivan, the day after the Revelation.* During this period Moses received the Torah, with its explanation and details of the precepts. He came down forty days later, on the seventeenth day of Tammuz, carrying the Tablets inscribed with the Ten Commandments. Finding the Golden Calf in the camp, he broke the Tablets, and on the following day he went up again on Mount Sinai to pray for G-d's forgiveness. On the day before Rosh Chodesh Elul, Moses returned, his prayers not fully answered. Finally, Moses went up on Mount Sinai for the third time. The forty days ended on the tenth day of Tishrei — *Yom Kippur* — when Moses came down,

---

* See COMPLETE STORY OF SHOVUOTH, by the author, published by Merkos L'Inyonei Chinuch, Inc.

bringing with him the second Tablets and the Divine message of forgiveness. Since then, our Sages tell us, the forty days from Rosh-Chodesh Elul until Yom-Kippur remained as days of special Divine grace and forgiveness, culminating in the Day of Atonement.

Thus, the sounding of the Shofar during the month of Elul is a call for repentance and preparation for the New Year. Being the last month of the year, it is the time for self-searching and spiritual stock-taking. The Shofar is therefore heard every morning on weekdays throughout the month of Elul, except on the day before Rosh-Hashanah. This interruption is made in order to distinguish between the sounding of the Shofar during Elul, which is a matter of custom and tradition, but not an express command in the Torah (hence no blessing is recited before sounding the Shofar during Elul), and the sounding of the Shofar on Rosh-Hashanah, which is the special precept of that festival, as expressly ordained in the Torah.

God is My Light

As a further reminder of the importance of this period, Psalm 27 is added to the daily prayers, morning and evening (at *Shacharith* and *Minchah* in some congregations; at *Shacharith* and *Maariv* in others).

A Psalm of David.

G-d is my light and salvation;
    Whom shall I fear?
G-d is the stronghold of my life;
    Of whom shall I be afraid?

"G-d is my light," our Sages explain, refers to Rosh-

Hashanah, "and my salvation," refers to the Day of Atonement. Our sincere return to G-d brings us both light and salvation.

Full of faith in G-d, the Psalmist expresses complete fearlessness in the face of all adversaries, both within and without. Freed from the burden of sins, he desires nothing more than the closeness of G-d.

> One thing I ask of G-d,
> One thing I desire:
> That I may dwell in the house of G-d
> All the days of my life;
> To behold the pleasantness of G-d,
> And to meditate in His sanctuary . . .

And the Psalmist concludes:

> Hope in G-d;
> Be strong
> And let your heart be brave —
> Yea, hope in G-d.

SELICHOTH

On the week before Rosh-Hashanah, the atmosphere of repentance is intensified by the addition of *Selichoth.*

Selichoth ("forgiveness") are special prayers for forgiveness, recited in the early hours of the morning (before the morning services) during the week before Rosh-Hashanah. The first *Selichoth* are introduced on Saturday night, preceding Rosh-Hashanah, usually immediately after midnight. If the first day of the festival occurs on Monday or Tuesday (it can never be on Sunday, Wednesday or Friday), the Selichoth are begun a week earlier.

The *Selichoth* are a very solemn reminder of the approach of Rosh-Hashanah. The Synagogue is crowded, and the air is charged with the solemnity of the occasion, and heightened by the special solemn tunes and melodies of the Days of Awe.

Happy New Year

From the first day of Elul the season of New Year greetings begins. It is customary to wish each other a Happy New Year, when greeting friends, or writing to them.

THE CONFESSION

Joseph and his younger brother Benny went with their father to the synagogue on the Saturday night before Rosh-Hashanah, for the special First Selichoth service. It was the first time that Benny went to the synagogue at such an unusual hour, for it was well past midnight. He had, however, managed to get some sleep that Sabbath afternoon, and was wide awake.

Benny was still too young to say the prayers, but he knew that "Selichoth" meant "forgiveness," and that everybody was praying to G-d for forgiveness. He stood, or sat, near his father and watched him all the time. He had never seen his father looking so serious before, especially when he was saying a certain prayer with his head bent down, at the same time touching his heart again and again with his right hand.

After the service, Benny asked his older brother about it. Joseph opened the prayer-book and showed him the prayer. "This is the prayer of Confession," he explained.

"What is confession?" asked Benny.

"Well, when you do something wrong and you say, 'I'm sorry I did this or that,' that is confession."

"What does this prayer say?"

"This prayer follows the Aleph-Beth. You see, '*Oshamnu*' begins with an *Aleph,* '*Bogdanu*' — with a *Beth,* and so on. These words mean, 'We have sinned,' 'We have been false,' 'We have robbed,' . . . But what's the matter, Benny? Why are you crying?"

"I thought father was the most wonderful man in the world. How could he do such things?!"

"Wait a minute! You don't really think *he* did these things, do you Benny?"

"Then, why did he say so? And he meant it, I watched him!"

Joseph could not help smiling. "Listen," he said, "and I'll explain it to you. This prayer is said by all Jews, even by the holiest Rabbis. You see, all Jews are like one body. When some part of the body hurts, the whole body is sick. When one Jew sins, he hurts our whole people. Therefore, the prayer mentions all possible sins, in the order of the *Aleph-Beth,* that *any* Jew, anywhere, may have done. That is why the prayer is '*We* have sinned,' that is, all together." And Joseph concluded:

"This goes to show how responsible we are for one another, and how we must always help each other to do only good."

Benny wiped his tears and felt much better, for he knew that his father was still the most wonderful man in the world, and he was praying not only for himself, but also for others.

SELICHOTH IN BERDITSCHEV

It was Erev-Rosh-Hashanah in Berditschev. The spirit of holiness hovered in the air. Each heart was throbbing with the thought of the imminent Day of Judgment; each mind was occupied with thoughts of repentance. The "balance sheet" of good deeds and misdeeds in the passing year did not quite tally; every one found himself "in the red." Too much time was wasted which could have been spent in the study of the Torah; perhaps more help should have been given to the poor, and how much of it was given from the pureness of the heart? And what about all that loose, and sometimes even mischievous, gossip? G-d only knows how many misdeeds, large and small, have accumulated during the year. It's high time to get wise. Well, thank G-d for the *Selichoth*. Here is a chance to pour out one's heart to G-d, the *last* opportunity to turn to G-d with real supplication, before the year is over. And the All-Merciful One will surely understand and forgive; for the new year will most definitely be a better one . . .

Such were the thoughts uppermost in everybody's mind, as the Jews of Berditschev hastily rose from their warm beds to go to the synagogue for the Selichoth of *Zechor Brith*. It was still very dark outside, for sunrise was hours away. They did not wait for the *Shamash* to knock them up on this last day of the year. As they hastened to the synagogue, the fresh autumn air drove the last vestiges of sleepiness from their eyes. They now met the Shamash, going on his beat, knocking with his long staff at the dark shutters of the stragglers who had overslept, and calling out, "Holy flock, arise to the service of G-d!" And soon enough the cracks in the shutters filled with light, for no one, but no one, was going to stay in bed on this solemn morning.

The narrow streets were soon filled with old men, and young men, and little boys of all ages. Many went to the *Mikvah* for immersion, and came out feeling purified and inspired. There were many visitors in Berditschev, who had come to spend the Solemn Days in the nearness of the saintly Rabbi Levi Yitzchak of Berditschev. They now made their way to the Rabbi's house, in order to accompany him to the synagogue. As they entered the Rabbi's home, they met him at the door, on his way out. They were amazed to see that he was holding a basket, from which the slim neck of a *vodka* bottle was sticking out invitingly. The tantalizing smell of freshly baked *kichlech* and fresh herring could not be ignored. "What on earth is the Rabbi going to do with the refreshments at this hour?" they wondered, as they followed him in silence at a respectful distance. Presently they approached the synagogue. The windows blazed with light, and you could see through the windows that the synagogue was already crowded with worshippers from wall to wall, waiting for the Rabbi.

But the Rabbi went past the synagogue! The wonder of his followers grew with every step. "Where was the Rabbi going? Was he so engrossed in meditation that he did not notice the synagogue?"

On and on the Rabbi strode, until almost to the outskirts of the town. The Rabbi was heading for the large inn, and his followers were close on his heels. Now he entered the inn, and his followers with him.

The large hall of the inn was filled with the smell of stale tobacco, and empty vodka bottles were strewn all over the place. On the floor, in the dimly lit hall, lay sleeping men, crowded like sardines: farmers, traders, wayfarers and beggars, many snoring in a medley of sonorous tones and whistles.

The Rabbi bent over a sleeping man, whose *Tzitzith*

were showing from under his *kaftan,* with his skull-cap hanging precariously on his head. He was a lean man, a bundle of bones held together by a pale skin which seemed ready to break at several points.

Gently the Rabbi woke him, whispering: "Reb Yid, your throat must be dry; you must have been snoring too long. Wake up, and take a gulp at this *schnapps;* I have a chaser,too: fresh herring and *kichlech,* a treat. . . ."

The Jew opened his eyes wide with amazement, threw a glance at the refreshments, but recoiled in horror. "I don't know you, my friend, but have you no G-d in your heart? Would I drink *mashke* before I've washed my hands? Would I eat before I have said my morning prayers? You must be joking. . . ."

The Rabbi moved on to the next sleeping Jew. Gently he shook him by his shoulders and repeated his offer in a most enticing way, but the reply was the same. The Rabbi fared no better with the third and fourth.

Then the Rabbi bent over a sleeping, corpulent country yokel. "Ivan, do you want a *schnapps* and some refreshments?"

Ivan rose quickly; the word "schnapps" acted like magic. "Give it here," he said, and he gulped down the glass of vodka in one shot. Eagerly he swallowed the piece of herring, and a *kichel,* which he ate with relish and licked his lips. "Thank you, pal," he murmured, and when no more was coming, he turned over on his other side and was soon snoring merrily again. The Rabbi moved on to the next sleeping farmer.

"Stepan, do you want a drink?" The story repeated itself, and once again the Rabbi was offering refreshments to other customers, until the basket was empty.

All was quiet, as the Berditschever Rabbi lifted his eyes to heaven and said, "Master of the Universe! Look at your children. Jacob gets up in the morning, and his

first thought is of Thee. He would not let anything pass his lips until he has sung Thy praises. But Esau's first thought is of food and drink. . . ."

His face beaming with satisfaction as his mission was accomplished, the Rabbi turned to his followers, "And now, holy flock, let's go to the house of G-d. We can now face our Maker with confidence, and pray for a happy New Year. . . ."

TWO STORIES

The Hole in the Boat

A man was called to the beach to paint a boat. He brought his paint and brush and began to paint the boat a bright new red, as he was engaged to do. As he painted the boat, he noticed that the paint was seeping through the bottom of the boat. He realized that there was a leak, and he decided to mend it. When the painting was done, he collected his money for the job and went away.

The following day the owner of the boat came to the painter and presented him with a big check. The painter was surprised. "You have already paid me for painting the boat," he said.

"But this is not for the paint job. It is for mending the leak in the boat."

"That was so small a thing that I even did not want to charge you for it. Surely you are not paying me this huge amount for so small a thing?"

"My dear friend, you do not understand. Let me tell you what happened.

"When I asked you to paint the boat I had forgotten to mention to you about the leak. When the boat was nice and dry, my children took the boat and went fishing. I wasn't home at the time. When I came home and found that they had gone out in the boat, I was frantic with fear for I remembered that the boat had a leak. Imagine my relief and happiness when I saw them coming back safe and sound. I examined the boat and saw that you had repaired the leak! Now you see what you have done? You have saved the lives of my children! I haven't enough money to repay you for your good 'little' deed. . . ."

A Piece of String

A wealthy merchant bought a wonderful candelabra for his home. It was a masterpiece of art, made of pure crystal and studded with precious stones. It cost a real fortune.

In order to hang up this beautiful candelabra, the merchant had a hole made in the ceiling. Through the hole he let one end of a rope drop into the living room which he attached to the candelabra. The other end of the rope he had fastened to a nail in the attic. Then he pulled the rope up until the candelabra was snugly hanging from the ceiling of his living room. The rest of the rope he wound around the nail in the attic.

Everybody who came to the house admired the wonderful candelabra, and the merchant and his household were very proud of it.

One day a poor boy came begging for old clothes. He was told to go up to the attic where old discarded clothes were stored, and help himself to some. This the poor beggar did. He collected a neat bundle of clothes, packed them in his bag, then looked for a piece of rope to tie up his bag. He saw a lot of rope wound around a nail and decided to help himself to a piece of rope. And so he took out his pocket knife and cut himself a piece of rope.

Crash! There was a terrific smash, and the next moment the whole family rushed to the attic crying, "You idiot! Look what you have done! You have cut the rope and have ruined us!"

The poor boy could not understand what all the excitement was about. Said he: "What do you mean, 'ruined' you? All I did was to take a small piece of rope. Surely this did not ruin you?"

"You poor fish," replied the merchant. "Yes, all you did was to take a piece of rope. But it so happened that my precious candelabra hung by it. Now you have broken it beyond repair!"

* * *

The two stories, my friends, have one moral. Very often, by doing what seems to us a "small" Mitzvah we never know what wonderful thing we have really done. And conversely, in committing what seems to us a "small" transgression, we are causing a terrible catastrophe. Both good deeds and bad deeds cause a "chain reaction." One good deed brings another good deed in its train, and one transgression brings another. Each of them, no matter how seemingly "small," may create or destroy worlds. Don't you think these two stories are worth remembering?

PSALMS FROM THE HEART

(A Story About the Baal-Shem-Tov)

It is an age-old custom to devote more time during the month of Elul to prayer and the reciting of T'hillim. Even scholarly Jews, who spend most of their time in the study of the Torah, devote more to prayer and T'hillim during these days.

In this connection, we bring you here the following story:

The saintly Baal-Shem-Tov was a great lover of his fellow-Jews. He loved the young ones and the old, the town-people and the country folk, the scholars and the unlearned. He loved them all with all his heart and soul.

No wonder Jews flocked to him from far and near, for isn't the heart like a mirror? As one feels towards the other, so does the other feel towards him. And so many Jews came to the Baal-Shem-Tov. Some came to listen to his words of Torah; to them the Baal-Shem-Tov revealed hidden secrets of the Torah which made their hearts sing for joy. Others, including the unlearned ones, came to ask his advice or blessing, or just to gaze at the saintly face of the Baal-Shem-Tov and to be inspired by the melodies they heard; for the melodies were sung without words, or with very simple words which they could understand.

The simple, unlearned folk felt very much ashamed of themselves for not having learned more in their youth. The Baal-Shem-Tov knew how they felt. He knew that it was not their fault. Indeed, he often told them that they must not feel unhappy, for G-d loves sincerity and simplicity and honesty and humility, and these were found in abundance among the unlearned. In this they were second to none!

To show them that he really meant it, the Baal-Shem-Tov was especially friendly and attentive to them. When he sat at the table, surrounded by his brilliant students, many of whom were famous scholars, the Baal-Shem-Tov invited the poor and simple folk to partake from the wine over which he had recited *Kiddush*, gave them generous slices of honey cake, and generally made them feel as though they were his favorite children.

The scholars who sat at the table could not understand why the saintly Baal-Shem-Tov was showering so much attention upon the unlearned folk.

The Baal-Shem-Tov also knew how the scholars felt. Once he told them: "You are surprised that I should favor the simple folks, arent you? It is true that they have not learned as much as you; some of them even do not know the meaning of the prayers they recite daily. But their hearts are of gold; their hearts are full to overflowing with love for humanity and for all of G-d's creatures, and they are humble and honest. They observe all the Mitzvoth of the Torah with simplicity and faith, even if they do not know much about them. Above all, there is a burning fire in their heart to be with G-d, like the Burning Bush that would not be consumed. How I envy their wonderful Jewish hearts!"

The students listened to their master and could hardly believe what they heard. The Baal-Shem-Tov looked at them earnestly and said, "I will show you soon that I have not exaggerated."

This was during the Third Repast (*Seudah shelishith*) of the holy Sabbath day. As was the custom, the Baal-Shem-Tov sat at the head of the table surrounded by his disciples. This was the occasion when he taught them secrets of the Torah. The simple folk who could not understand the mysteries of the Torah would at that time retire to an adjoining room, where they would recite the Psalms of King David as best as they could.

The Baal-Shem-Tov closed his eyes and became deeply engrossed. His holy face showed deep concentration, and beads of perspiration stood out on his brow. Suddenly, his face lit up with a great inner joy. He opened his eyes and all his disciples felt as though they bathed in his happiness. The Baal-Shem-Tov turned to his disciple sitting at his right: "Place your right hand on the shoulder of your neighbor." He ordered the next one to do the same, and the next, until they all formed a chain. Then he ordered them to sing a certain melody which they sang only on the most solemn occasions. "Sing with all your heart, as you have never sung before," he said. And as they sang, they felt their hearts rising higher and higher.

When they finished singing, the Baal-Shem-Tov placed his right hand on the shoulder of the disciple on his right, and his left hand on the shoulder of his disciple on his left. Now the human chain was closed.

"Let's close our eyes and concentrate," the Baal-Shem-Tov said.

Presently they heard many wonderful, melodious voices, singing Psalms. The voices were so sweet and moving that they felt as if all their heartstrings were being pulled in wonderful rhythm. Some of the voices expressed unshakable faith, others were full of joyous abandon, still others expressed heart-rending appeal. They could clearly distinguish the saintly words of the Psalms with which they were so familiar, and the frequent exclamations with which the words were intermingled: "Oh, Heavenly Father!" or "Oh, Sweet Father in Heaven!" or "Oh, Master of the Universe!"

The circle of disciples that had joined with the Baal-Shem-Tov into this heavenly excursion, sat spellbound, in complete silence. They had lost all sense of time and

place; tears flowed from their closed eyes, and their hearts were full of ecstasy, ready to burst.

Suddenly, the singing stopped, for the Baal-Shem-Tov had removed his arms and broken the chain. It was not a moment too soon, for the next moment the souls of the disciples would have surely left their bodies.

When they recovered from their soul-stirring experience, the Baal-Shem-Tov told them how much G-d likes to listen to the Psalms, especially when they come straight from the heart, and more especially when they come straight from the pure hearts of the simple, honest and humble folk.

"But whose voices did we hear a little while ago?" asked the disciples. And they were amazed indeed when the Baal-Shem-Tov replied:

"You were listening for one brief moment to the Psalms recited by the simple folk in the *next room*, as the angels in heaven hear them!"

THE MONTH OF TISHREI IN JEWISH HISTORY

The month of Tishrei is the seventh month in the Jewish Calendar. This may seem strange, since Rosh-Hashanah, the New Year, is on the first and second day of Tishrei. The reason is that the Torah made the month of Nissan the first month of the year, in order to emphasize the historic importance of the liberation from Egypt, which took place on the 15th day of that month, and which marked the birth of our Nation. However, according to tradition, the world was created in Tishrei, or, more exactly, Adam and Eve were created on the first day of Tishrei, which was the sixth day of Creation, and it is from Tishrei that the annual cycle began. Hence, Rosh-Hashanah is celebrated at this time.

* * *

There are twelve months in the year, and there are twelve Tribes in Israel. Every month of the Jewish year has its representative Tribe. The month of Tishrei is the month of the Tribe of *Dan*. This is of symbolic significance, for when Dan was born, his mother Leah said, "G-d has *judged* me (*dannani*) and also hearkened to my voice." *Dan* and *Din* (*Yom-haDin*—Day of Judgment) are thus both derived from the same root, symbolizing that Tishrei is the time of Divine judgment and forgiveness.

Similarly, every month of the Jewish Calendar has its sign of the Zodiak (in Hebrew—*Mazal*). The sign of the Zodiak for Tishrei is *Scales*. This is symbolic of the Day of Judgment, when G-d *weighs* the good deeds and the bad deeds of man.

* * *

Although every New Moon is announced and blessed in the synagogue on the Sabbath preceding it, the New Moon of Tishrei is neither announced nor blessed in the synagogue. It is not blessed by us, because G-d Himself blesses it. It is not announced, because much about Rosh-Hashanah is "concealed" and shrouded in mystery. The mystical aspect of Rosh-Hashanah is indicated in Scripture, "Sound the Shofar on the New Moon, in *concealment* of the day of our festival" (Ps. 81:4-5). Satan, the Accuser, is not to be given notice about the arrival of Rosh-Hashanah, the Day of Judgment. This is also one of the reasons why the "New Moon" is not mentioned in the prayers of Rosh-Hashanah. It is also one of the reasons why the first portion of Genesis is not read on Rosh-Hashanah, although it would have been appropriate to read it, since Rosh-Hashanah is the birthday of Man, for Adam was created on Rosh-Hashanah (*see below*).

* * *

The first day of Tishrei, that is the first day of Rosh-Hashanah, can never occur on Sunday, Wednesday, or Friday.

Historically, however, the first Rosh-Hashanah occurred on Friday, the sixth day of Creation. On this day, G-d first created the beasts of the field and of the woods, and all the creeping things and insects, and, lastly—Man. Thus, when man was created, he found everything in readiness for him. Our Sages saw in this order of Creation the thoughtfulness of a good host who, before inviting an honored guest, gets the home in order, prepares bright lights, good food, etc., so that the guest would find everything prepared for him. But they see in it also a profound lesson: If man is worthy, he is treated like an honored guest; if he is unworthy, he is told: "Don't be proud of yourself; even an insect was created before you!"

Adam, the first man, was created in his full stature. He was a very intelligent being, and the moment he opened his eyes, he recognized his Creator and proclaimed Him "King of the Universe." And he called upon all creation: "Come, let us worship, bow down and kneel before G-d, our Maker!" Thus, Rosh-Hashanah is the Day of Coronation of the King of the Universe, and as the coronation of kings is heralded by the sounding of trumpets, so the sounding of the Shofar on Rosh-Hashanah symbolically reminds us also of the Divine Coronation. For the same reason, this day is a day of "amnesty" and forgiveness.

* * *

On the very first day of his creation, Adam transgressed G-d's command, by eating from the forbidden tree, and he was judged by G-d. It teaches us that it is human to err, but Divine to forgive."

On the day of Rosh-Hashanah Cain was born, together with a twin-sister. Abel, was also born on the day of Rosh-Hashanah, together with a twin-sister.

It was also on Rosh-Hashanah that Cain killed his brother Abel, but repented immediately. On learning of the power of repentance, Adam, too, repented. (*See The First Repenters*, p. 33).

* * *

According to one opinion, the waters of the Flood dried up on Rosh-Hashanah. The same opinion holds that our Patriarchs, Abraham, Isaac and Jacob, were all born on Rosh-Hashanah and died on this day. We read about the birth of Isaac on the first day of Rosh-Hashanah, and about the Binding of Isaac (*Akedah*) on the second day.

* * *

Our Matriarchs Sarah and Rivkah, and also the prophetess Hannah, who were childless, were blessed with offspring as their prayers were answered on Rosh-Hashanah.

* * *

Other events in our ancient history took place on Rosh-Hashanah: The prophet Elisha blessed the woman of Shunem with having a child; the returned exiles from Babylon began to offer sacrifices to G-d once more; Ezra the Scribe gathered all the people and read to them portions from the Torah, arousing a great spirit of repentance among the returned exiles. However, Ezra and Nehemiah told the people not to have sadness or grief on the festival, but postpone their fasting and tears for after Succoth.

During the Middle Ages, in the year 4773, Rabbi Amnon died a martyr's death on the first day of Rosh-Hashanah; he is the author of the solemn prayer "*Unesaneh toikef,*" recited during the *Musaph* service of Rosh-Hashanah and Yom-Kippur. (See p. 64.)

* * *

The second day of Tishrei was, at the time of Creation, the Sabbath, the *first* Sabbath. At the termination of the Sabbath, Adam and Eve saw darkness for the first time. Frightened, they sat in darkness until Adam chanced upon two stones which he struck against each other to produce a spark of light. He then pronounced the blessing over light. (That is why it is said at *Habdalah* every Saturday night.)

According to some authorities, Gedaliah, the son of Ahikam, the Governor of Judea after the destruction of the first Beth-Hamikdosh, was assassinated on the second day of Rosh-Hashanah, at Mitzpah (in the year 3339). The Fast of Gedaliah is observed on the following day, however, on account of the festival.

* * *

The third day of Tishrei is observed as the Fast of Gedaliah (see above). With his assassination the remnants of the Jewish settlement in the Holy Land suffered a grievous blow. It is one of the Four Fasts connected with the Destruction of the Beth-Hamikdosh.

* * *

On the *fourth day* of Tishrei (in the year 5474), the

saintly man and mystic, Rabbi Joel Baal-Shem of Ostrah, died. On the same day (in the year 5581) died Rabbi Abraham the son of Yehiel Michel of Wilno, author of the famous books on Jewish laws and customs *Haye-Adam* and *Hochmath-Adam.*

* * *

The *fifth day* of Tishrei is the birthday of Naftali, the son of our Patriarch Jacob. He lived for 133 years, and died, according to one opinion, on the same day.

On this day, also, Rabbi Akiba was arrested by the Romans, and he died a martyr's death at their hands on the day of Yom-Kippur. He was one of the Ten Martyrs who were slain by the Romans.

* * *

The *sixth day* of Tishrei is the Yahrzeit of the "Grandfather of Spola," who passed away in the year 5572.

* * *

On the *seventh* day of Tishrei, Zebulun, the son of our Patriarch Jacob was born. He lived for 110 years (according to another opinion, Zebulun lived for 124 years).

* * *

On the *eighth* day of Tishrei, the dedication of the Beth-Hamikdosh, built by King Solomon (in the year 2935 after creation), began. From that day on, no sacrifices were permitted to be offered elsewhere.

* * *

The *ninth* day of Tishrei is *Erev Yom Kippur.*

* * *

The tenth day of Tishrei is Yom Kippur, the Day of Atonement. It cannot occur on Sunday, Tuesday, or Friday.

It was on this day that our Patriarch Abraham circumcised himself at the age of 99 years (in the year 2047 after Creation). (According to another opinion it took place on the second day of Rosh-Hashanah; and a third opinion holds that it was on the 13th day of Nissan).

On Yom-Kippur (in the year 2449, the year after the Exodus), Moses came down from Mount Sinai, carrying the second Tablets of stone with the Ten Commandments, with the happy tidings of G-d's forgiveness (for the transgression of the Golden Calf).

During the celebration of the dedication of the Beth Hamikdosh of King Solomon (*the eighth day, above*), there was no fasting on Yom-Kippur, by special Divine injunction; but it was devoted to the celebration of the great event.

Rabbi Akiba (as mentioned above) died a martyr's death on Yom-Kippur, with the words of the *Shema* on his lips. On the day of his death, Rabbi Judah the Prince (compiler of the Mishnah) was born.

On Yom-Kippur, Emperor Hadrian issued a decree forbidding circumcision. (Ca. 4260-4300 after Creation).

Rabbi Ahai, the son of Rava bar Abuha, of the *Rabbanan Seburai,* died on Yom Kippur.

THE NEW YEAR

ROSH HASHANAH

EW YEAR's day is for us Jews not a time for frivolous rejoicing, but rather a solemn day of prayer. It is the Day of Memorial when all creatures of the earth are remembered by the Creator and judged according to their merits.

Yet, solemn and awe-inspiring though this day is, we know that the Supreme Judge of the universe is kind and merciful. He is not out to punish us, but merely wants us to follow the laws and regulations He laid down for us for our own good. He has made this day of Judgment a day of forgiveness and mercy.

Rosh-Hashanah does not find us unprepared. In the month of Elul the approach of Rosh-Hashanah was heralded by the daily sounding of the Shofar in the synagogue (except Saturdays).*) During the month of Elul the Jew is particularly careful in the observance of the religious precepts; he takes more time for his prayers; he finds himself overflowing with charitableness and loving-kindness, and resolutely determines to cast away his evil ways and habits of the past. And a wonderful feeling grips the heart of the true repenter, as if a magic hand has removed the heavy burden that has been weighing upon it in the past. It is the feeling of being able to begin life anew, like a newly-born innocent child, with no blemish on his record.

Such is the feeling that the Jew brings with him into the synagogue on the first night of Rosh-Hashanah. He finds himself close to G-d, with his prayers pouring out from the very depth of his heart.

---

* See page 3.

The Book of Life

Coming home from *shul* we greet the members of our family with an affectionate "Good-yomtov, l'shono toivo tikoseiv v'sechoseim!" (may you be inscribed unto a happy year). Saying this, we can almost see the three huge Divine ledgers laid open before G-d: the Book of the Righteous—no, we wouldn't be there, for it contains a very few exclusive names; the Book of the Wicked—we wouldn't be there either, thank G-d; and the Book of the Average—that's where we are likely to be, with our good deeds and bad deeds just about cancelling each other out. Just one more Mitzvah, and the balance is in our favor! Why, we might even tip the scale in favor of the whole of mankind, assuming that the wicked and the good people are fifty-fifty. What a lofty thought our Sages suggested!

The Honey

Kiddush is recited in that heart-warming tune, and the hands are washed before the festive Rosh-Hashanah meal. Then comes the charming custom of dipping the bread in honey, followed by the dipping of a piece of sweet apple in honey, with the recital of the short prayer: "May it be Thy will—to renew unto us a good and sweet year." (Not forgetting first to make the blessing over the apple, of course). Various traditional foods such as fish, the head of a lamb, carrots, etc., are served on the night of Rosh-Hashanah, symbolic of innocence, merits and good fortune.

On the second night of Rosh-Hashanah there is invariably that new fruit that the children always look forward to, which is tasted for the first time in the season, so that the blessing "Sheheheyanu" might be made over it.

The Morning Service

The morning service on Rosh-Hashanah begins early as there's a lot to pray, and the Shofar must be sounded.

The prayers are said with the same ardent sincerity as on the night before. Then we listen to the reading of the Torah, chanted in that special tune which we hear only on Rosh-Hashanah and Yom-Kippur. It's a moving story: The birth of Isaac—a belated but wonderful gift to the aged Abraham and Sarah; what great rejoicing! It's the first occasion of initiating a Jewish boy into the covenant of Abraham with G-d! The loving and kind Abraham sees himself compelled to send away Hagar and Ishmael. . . Ishmael's peril and rescue; his settling down in the desert as a hunter, with archery as his trade, while Isaac devotes his life to the study of the Torah and the service of G-d . . . The mighty king Abimelech of Gerar seeks Abraham's friendship . . . Abraham erects a free hostel in Beer-Sheba and teaches all wayfarers to worship the osly G-d, the Creator of the Universe. . . .

Even more moving and inspiring is the reading of the Torah on the second day of Rosh-Hashanah. It is the story of the "Akedah" (the binding of Isaac)—the severest test that any father and son were ever called upon to go through, and which both passed unflinchingly, with equal devotion and loyalty to G-d. The story is too well known to be repeated here.

The Shofar

After reading the Torah, the most solemn moment arrives—the Shofar is about to be sounded!

The Baal-Tokeah in his *kittle* (white robe, symbolizing purity) is getting ready to sound the Shofar. For a little while there is silence in the crowded *shul* whilst everybody is preoccupied with himself, as this is a most suitable moment for self-examination and final repentance.

Many thoughts flash through our mind about the significance of the sounding of the Shofar: Of course, it's a commandment like any other commandment of the Torah, but it drives home many important messages to us:

To begin with, it is like the sound of the bugle, or "Reveille," rousing the sleeping soldiers to their duties. The Shofar calls unto us: "Wake up! Wake up! There's work to be done! You have been lulled into mental lethargy by unimportant earthly things; you have neglected your spiritual needs! Wake up now! Give your soul a chance, too!"

The sound of the Shofar is an "alert," as our prophet Amos says: "Shall the Shofar be sounded in the city and the people not tremble?" The sound of the Shofar inspires us with awe, for it reminds us that it is a Day of Judgment.

The broken sounds of the "Shevarim" and "Teruah" are like stifled sobs and groans, piercing the heart; they break the heart with remorse for our past failings. . . .

The "Tekiah Gedolah" — the last long blast of the Shofar — strikes a more cheerful note, however, for it reminds us of That Great Day when the Great Shofar will be sounded to gather all the exiles of our people Israel, like a shepherd gathering in his flocks, and when with our Righteous Messiah at our head, we will return to the Land of Israel. . . .

From our reflections on the sound of the Shofar we pass on to think of the Shofar itself. The Shofar is a ram's horn. It reminds us of the Ram that was sacrificed by Abraham in Isaac's place. The story of the "Akedah" (the binding of Isaac) which we read on the second day of Rosh-Hashanah comes back to our mind with its full force. We are proud of being the children of Abraham and Isaac, and to have inherited some of their undaunted loyalty and devotion to G-d. G-d couldn't be very angry with the children of Abraham, Isaac and Jacob, who, in their time, were the first and only ones to proclaim G-d's name to the world! The more we think of our great ancestors, the more we feel inspired by their great deeds. We realize that true devotion to our Torah and our G-d means being prepared to make sacrifices, and being absolutely selfless. We know that thousands, nay, millions of our brethren have faced death with undaunted courage for the sanctification of G-d's Name, like Abraham and Isaac. How far would *we* go?

Tashlich

After the service we go home to eat. There is no afternoon nap on Rosh-Hashanah, as is often the case on Shabbos after "*tcholent.*" Time is too precious on Rosh-Hashanah. No sooner are we through with our meal than we go back to *shul*. On the first day of Rosh-Hashanah *Mincha* is *davvened* early because of *Tashlich,* and besides, we want to say as many Psalms as we can manage. Some manage to say the whole book of Psalms over and over again during the two days of Rosh-Hashanah. Children vie with each other as to who said more Psalms. . . .

One *minyan* after another *davvens Mincha* as people come in and go off to *Tashlich*. We *davven Mincha* and join a company of young and old members of our synagogue walking to the nearest park where there's a lake. We fetch a *machzor* with us.

There by the bank of the lake we find lots of Jews from various congregations, young and old, and some truly venerable-looking. There are also many Jewish women there, all saying the *Tashlich* prayers, and many of them wiping a tear off their faces. Some worshippers have completed saying *Tashlich* and they are shaking the corners of their garments, as if they were finally dumping all their sins into the water. This is symbolic of the words of the prophet, Micah: " . . . and Thou shalt throw into the depth of the sea all their sins. . . ."

Of course, the mere shaking of the corners of our garments will not shake off the sins. But it does remind us that we must give our heart a thorough cleaning and rid it of all evil. And indeed there is a feeling in our hearts after Tashlich as if we have left a heavy burden behind. It's a comforting feeling, and it helps us carry out our good resolutions for the New Year.

THE CORONATION

It was late on the Sixth Day since G-d began the Creation of the World. Everything was now ready, or *almost* everything. The sun shone brightly in the blue sky, and its rays playfully flickered in the clear waters of the rivers, brooks, and lakes down below. The meadows were green with fresh grass. The birds twittered happily in the air. The woods were full of squirrels, and rabbits, and all kinds of big and small animals.

But all the animals were dumb, and had no sense to know how they came to be, and who created them. And so G-d decided to create the last, and most wonderful creature, a creature who would be able to think, and talk, and do wonderful things. This creature was Man.

When Adam opened his eyes and saw the beautiful world around him, he knew at once that G-d created the world, and him, too. Adam's first words were: "The

Lord is King forever and ever!" and the echo of his voice rang through the world.

"Now the whole world will know that I am King," G-d said, and He was very pleased.

This was the *first* Rosh-Hashanah! The first New Year. It was the birthday of Man, and the Coronation Day of the King of kings!

"Now, let's see what do kings do on their Coronation Day?" G-d asked, and He answered: "They make that day a festival. The loyal subjects gather everywhere to express their love and loyalty to the king. They sound the trumpets and call out 'Long live the King!' The king is filled with love for his subjects, and grants them many favors and honors. He even forgives the bad men who acted against his wishes, if they feel sorry. Yes, that's what kings do on their Coronation Day. That's what I will do!"

And so G-d made Rosh Hashanah a holy festival. We gather in the synagogues, sound the Shofar, and express our love for our King and Father in heaven. And G-d is very pleased and kind to all of us, and grants us a happy New Year.

THE FIRST REPENTERS

According to tradition, it was on Rosh-Hashanah that Cain slew his brother Abel.

Abel lay motionless on the ground. Cain realized that he had killed his brother. "What shall I do with his body?" he thought, completely at a loss, for he had not seen a dead body before, nor did he know what to do with it.

Loud and angry twittering sounds made him raise his eyes. He saw two ravens fighting fiercely. Presently, one of them fell to the ground and lay still, lifeless like his brother. The victorious bird began to dig a hole in the ground with its beak and claws. It rolled the body of the dead bird into it, covered it with soil and flew away.

Cain now knew what he had to do. He dug a grave in the ground and lay the body of his brother into it and covered it with soil. "I must run away from here," he thought. Then he heard a heavenly voice, "Do you think you can run away from Me? Where is your brother Abel?"

Cain became frightened. "I know not," he replied. "Am I my brother's keeper?"

"You foolish son of man," G-d said to him again. "You cannot hide anything from Me!"

Cain's heart was filled with remorse. He was deeply sorry for what he had done. "Is my sin too heavy even for Divine forgiveness?" he cried in anguish.

G-d looked into Cain's heart, and saw that he was truly sorry. Said G-d, "Because you have repented honestly, with all your heart, I will lighten your punishment. I will spare your life, but a restless vagabond and wanderer you shall be to the end of your days; then you, too, will die at the hands of a man."

Cain set out on his wanderings. His father Adam met him. "Why are you so sad, my son?" Adam asked him. Cain told him all that had happened.

"Is the power of repentance so great?" Adam exclaimed. "What a pity I did not know it sooner."

Adam now prayed to G-d to forgive him for his own sin of eating from the forbidden tree. He prayed with all his heart, and G-d accepted his sincere repentance, and forgave him.

Cain and Adam were the first repenters. They repented, and were forgiven—on Rosh-Hashanah.

ROSH HASHANAH IN BERDITSCHEV

It was the first day of Rosh-Hashanah in the synagogue of the Berditschever Rabbi, Rabbi Levi Yitzchak.

The synagogue was crowded. The Berditschever Rabbi himself was at the *Amud,* leading the congregation in the solemn prayers.

"All declare Thy Majesty, O G-d, Who sittest in Judgment. . . ."

The Rabbi's soft, vibrant voice touched the heartstrings of every worshipper. Hardly anybody's eyes were dry. From the women's gallery many a sob burst forth, loud enough to send the tears rolling down every face.

"To Him, Who searches the hearts in the Day of Judgment. . . ."

As the Rabbi pronounced the words, his voice broke, and everybody's heart was filled with remorse. Everybody pictured himself standing before the Seat of Glory, where the Judge of the whole Universe presided, to dispense justice, and to pronounce the verdict. "Be merciful and gracious to us," was the inaudible plea, coming from the innermost recesses of every heart.

The Rabbi recited line after line of the solemn prayer, which the congregation repeated, until he came to the line:

"To Him, Who acquires His servants in judgment..."

Here the Rabbi suddenly paused, for the words died on his lips. His prayer shawl (*Tallith*) slid from his head onto his shoulders, revealing his pale face; his eyes were shut, and he seemed to be in a trance.

A shudder passed through the worshippers. Something was amiss. A critical situation must have arisen in the Heavenly Court; things were not going well for the petitioners. The Prosecution was apparently on the verge of triumph. . . . Only increased prayer and repentance could change the ominous verdict. . . . The congregation of worshippers held its breath, and waited with palpitating hearts.

A few moments later, the Rabbi suddenly came to. The color returned to his face, which now became radiant with joy. His voice shook with ecstasy and triumph as he recited:

"To Him, who acquires His servants in judgment!"

After the service, when the Rabbi was sitting at his festive table, surrounded by his ardent followers, one of the elders plucked up courage to enquire of the Rabbi as to what caused the interruption in his prayer, and why precisely at those words.

The Rabbi began to relate:

— I felt myself lifted up to the gates of heaven, and then I saw Satan carrying a heavy load. The sight filled me with anxiety, for I knew that the Unholy one was carrying a bagful of sins to put onto the Scales of Justice before the Heavenly Court. Suddenly Satan put the bag down and hastened in a downward swoop—no doubt to pick up yet another sin, committed by some hapless Jew on this very Solemn Day. The bag having been left unattended, I went up to it and began to examine its contents. The bag was crammed with all kinds of sins: evil gossip, hatred without reason, jealousies, wasted time which should have been spent in study of the Torah, thoughtless prayers, and so on—ugly creatures of sins, big and small. And while I was wondering what to do, I knew that even at that very moment the One With a Thousand Eyes had spied yet another sin, and would soon bring it gleefully to put into the bag. "Dear me," I thought, "things don't look too good." I pushed my hand into the bag and began pulling out one sin after another, to look at it more closely. I saw that almost all the sins were committed unwillingly, without pleasure, downright carelessly, or in sheer ignorance. No Jew was really bad, but the circumstances of exile, poverty and hardships, sometimes harden his heart, set his nerves on edge, bring about petty jealousies, and the like.

And strangely enough, as I was examining all these sins, and thinking what was really behind them, they seemed to melt away, one by one, until hardly anything was left in the bag. The bag dropped back, limp and empty. . . .

The next moment, I heard a terrible cry. Satan was back, and discovering what I had done, he was filled with anger and consternation. "You thief! What did you do to my sins?" He grabbed at my beard and *peyoth,* yelling, "Thief, Robber. All year I labored to gather these precious sins, and now you have stolen them! You shall pay double!"

"How can I pay you?" I pleaded. "My sins may be many, but not *so* many."

"Well, you know the Law," the Adversary countered. "He who steals must pay double, and if he is unable to pay, he shall be sold into servitude. You are my slave now! Come!"

The thought of being Satan's slave chilled my blood, and I was ready to collapse.

Finally, my captor brought me before the Seat of Glory, and pleaded his case before the Supreme Judge of the Universe.

After listening to Satan's complaint, the Holy One, blessed is He, said: "*I* will buy him, for so I promised through my prophet Isaiah (46:4): Even to his old age, I will be the same, and when he is grey-headed, still will I sustain him. I have made him, I will bear him, I will sustain and save him!"

At this point I came to — concluded the Berditschever Rabbi. — Now I understand the meaning of the words,

"To Him, who acquires His servants in Judgment!" We are the servants of G-d, and if we are faithful servants, G-d protects us and is our Merciful Master. Let us remain faithful servants to G-d, and we'll be spared from being servants of servants, and in the merit of this, the Almighty will surely inscribe us all in the Book of Life, for a happy New Year.

READINGS FROM THE TORAH ON ROSH HASHANAH

First Day:

Portion: GENESIS xxi

Haphtorah: I SAMUEL, i

Five men are called up to the reading of the Torah on Rosh-Hashanah, if it occurs on a week-day; seven—if the first day occurs on a Sabbath; in both cases—apart from the one called up to *Maftir*. Two scrolls are taken out; the second one is for Maftir.

The birth of Isaac is the theme of the reading of the Torah on the first day of Rosh-Hashanah.*)

* See page 21.

The message of the portion may be found in a number of lessons. First, there is the lesson of Divine Providence and Omnipotence. Sarah, at the age of ninety, gives birth to her first and only child, Isaac, the second of our Patriarchs, when Abraham was one hundred years old. Isaac is entered into the Covenant of our father Abraham at the age of eight days, as G-d had commanded.

The importance of upbringing and education is also emphasized in this portion. Seeing that Ishmael, Isaac's elder half-brother, the son of Hagar, exercises a bad influence on the younger Isaac, Sarah insists on sending away both Hagar and her son. Lost in the desert of Beer-Sheba and on the brink of a painful death from thirst, Divine Providence saves Ishmael by a miraculous revelation of a well.

The portion concludes with an episode illustrating Abraham's rise in the eyes of the surrounding neighbors, when Abimelech, king of the Philistines, comes to visit Abraham to conclude a covenant of peace with him.

The birth of Samuel is the theme of the Haphtorah. Both Sarah and Hannah had been childless and barren, but G-d eventually blessed them each with a son. Both Isaac and Samuel were consecrated to the service of G-d: Isaac through the *Akedah* (Binding), and Samuel as a prophet.

The Haphtorah concludes with the significant words: "O Lord! G-d's adversaries shall be broken when from heaven G-d will thunder down upon them and judge the ends of the world; He will give strength to His king and raise the horn of His anointed." Here the prophetess Hannah refers to the final Day of Judgment and the "horn of Messiah,"—a theme which we mention many times in our prayers of this day.

Second Day:

Haphtorah: Jeremiah 31

Portion: Genesis xxii

The "Binding of Isaac" (*Akedah*) is the theme of the reading in the Torah, on the second day of Rosh-Hashanah, which directly follows the portion of the previous day. It is the symbol of self-sacrifice with which we, the children of Abraham, are always ready to obey G-d's commands, and for which G-d has promised us His blessings.

The Haphtorah suitably speaks of the final rebuilding and redemption of Israel: "For the Lord hath redeemed Jacob, and ransomed him from a hand too strong for him . . . Thus saith the Lord: Refrain thy voice from weeping, and thine eyes from tears, for thy work shall be rewarded . . . and they shall return from the land of the enemy. And there is hope for thy future . . . and thy children shall return to their own border." The Haphtorah concludes with G-d's moving declaration of His everlasting love and mercy for Israel: "Surely Ephraim is My own darling child! For whenever I speak of him, I do earnestly remember him still. . . . I will surely have mercy upon him, saith the Lord."

HANNAH

Hannah was one of the seven women to whom G-d gave the power of prophecy, for altogether we had seven women prophetesses, and forty-eight prophets, whose prophecies are mentioned in the TeNaCh.

The story, as we read it on Rosh Hashonah from the first chapter of the book of Samuel I, begins with introducing to us Elkanah, Hannah's husband. He was a Levite (belonging to the tribe of Levi) and lived in Ramathaim-Zophim of Mount Ephraim. Elkanah was a man of noble character and of great piety. He saw with sorrow that many of his Jewish brethren were slowly drifting away from G-d, and he took upon himself to create a lively interest in the spiritual center of Shiloh, where Eli the High Priest was the Judge of Israel in those days. As prescribed in the Torah, Elkanah made a pilgrimage to Shiloh during each of the Three Festival seasons. Together with him his family spent the holiday in a religious atmosphere in the holy city of the Sanctuary. When the people saw Elkanah's caravan making its way to Shiloh in a happy and festive spirit, many of them joined him. A closer bond thus developed between the Jewish people and their spiritual center in Shiloh, thanks to Elkanah's influence.

Hannah was one of the two wives of Elkanah, and she was childless. Silently she suffered many humiliations at the hands of the more fortunate Peninah, who did have children. On one of the annual pilgrimages to Shiloh, Hannah stood in the Sanctuary and poured out her heart before G-d. She prayed that G-d bless her with a son, and vowed that she would consecrate his whole life to G-d. Silently she prayed, swaying slightly. Eli saw her and thought she was drunk. He rebuked her for entering the Sanctuary in a state of drunkenness. But Hannah answered with dignity, "No, my lord, I am a woman of a sorrowful spirit; I have drunk neither wine nor strong drink, but have poured out my soul before G-d." Eli realized the deep piety and grief which had moved this woman, and he said to her, "Go in peace, and the G-d of Israel grant thee thy petition which thou hast asked of Him." Hannah thanked him graciously and went away with happiness in her heart, feeling certain that her prayer was accepted.

In due time a son was born to her, whom she named Samuel, meaning, as she said, "I have asked him (borrowed him) of G-d." Hannah's joy knew no bounds. The first few years she kept him home. Then true to her promise, she took him to Shiloh with an offering of gratitude to G-d. Turning the boy over to Eli, the High Priest, Hannah said, "My lord . . . I am the woman that stood by thee here praying unto G-d. For this child I prayed, and G-d hath given me my petition." She told Eli of her vow, and left her beloved son in Eli's care, to be brought up in a wholly religious atmosphere in the Sanctury.

You might think that Hannah would be heart-broken to part with her son, for whom she had prayed for so many years. But Hannah was full of joy as she prayed to G-d and said, "My heart rejoices in G-d." These were the first words of Hannah's famous prophecy which reads like a wonderful hymn: "There is none holy as G-d, for there's none beside Thee; neither is there any rock like our G-d.

"Talk no more so exceedingly proudly; let not arrogance come out of your mouth;

"For G-d is an all-knowing G-d; and unto Him all actions are known.

"G-d bringeth death and maketh alive; He bringeth down to the grave, and He bringeth up.

"G-d maketh poor, and maketh rich; He bringeth low, and He lifteth up.

"He raiseth up the poor out of the dust, and lifteth

up the beggar from the dunghill, to set them among princes, to make them inherit the seat of glory. . . ."

As we read the inspiring words of the prophetess, we can see at once how fitting they are for the Day of Judgment, Rosh-Hashanah, when G-d decides on the fate of each person: who shall live, who shall be rich, who shall be honored — or otherwise.

Our Sages tell us that the prophetess Hannah has taught us several important things. One of them is the importance of reciting prayer in a whisper. As you know, we have the "quiet" *Shemone-Esrei,* which is then repeated aloud by the Chazzan (if the service is held in the synagogue). The "quiet" Shemone-Esrei, which we say in a whisper, our lips moving but our voice hardly audible, in the way Hannah prayed, is the most important part of our prayer. When the heart is full and overwhelmed in the presence of the Almighty, then prayer is best expressed in a whisper.

Hannah also introduced the holy name of G-d, as the "G-d of Hosts," that is, the Master of the whole universe, the hosts of heaven and earth. It is most fitting on Rosh-Hashanah, when we proclaim G-d's kingdom over the whole world.

According to the Targum (which reveals many secrets hidden in the Holy Scriptures), the first verse of Hannah's prayer contains the prophecy that her son Samuel would be a prophet in Israel; that in his days the people of Israel would be delivered from the Philistines; that he would perform many miracles and wonders; and that his grandson Heyman with his fourteen sons would sing and say Psalms in the Beth-Hamikdosh, together with other fellow Levites. In the second verse, Hannah predicts the defeat of Sennacherib at the gates of Jerusalem. Further on she prophesies about Nebuchadnezzar and other enemies of Israel who would pay for their wickedness; among them the Macedonians (Greeks) who would be defeated by the Hasmoneans;* the wicked Haman and his sons and their defeat at the hands of Mordecai and Esther.** Finally, Hannah also prophesies about the great world war, when all the world will be engulfed in a desperate war of self-extermination, and then the Messiah will come and bring complete redemption to the people of Israel, and there will be a new world in which there will be no evil, no destruction, for all the world will be full of the wisdom of G-d.

He who says, I will sin and repent—will not be given an opportunity to repent.

He who says, I will sin and Yom Kippur will forgive—will not be forgiven on Yom Kippur.

Transgressions against a fellow-man are not forgiven on Yom Kippur unless the offended person is first reconciled. This is what Rabbi Elazar ben Azariah said: It is written, "Of all your sins *before G-d* you will be cleansed." (*Lev.* 16:30) Yom-Kippur forgives only sins against G-d, while sins against a fellow-man are not forgiven until forgiveness is obtained from the person offended.

Said Rabbi Akiba: You happy Israelites! Before Whom do you cleanse yourselves and Who cleanses you?—Your Father in Heaven!

(*Talmud Babli,* Yoma 85b)

---

* See COMPLETE STORY OF CHANUKAH, by the author.

** See COMPLETE STORY OF PURIM, by the author.

The Shofar

The Shofar, as you all know, is a plain ram's horn. All year round it is hidden away somewhere in the Holy Ark in the synagogue, or in another suitable place, and we do not give it a thought. But when the month of Elul comes, the Shofar emerges from its hiding place to play a very prominent part during the Solemn Days. Blowing of the Shofar (*Tekiath Shofar*) highlights the service of Rosh-Hashanah, and it makes a final appearance at the conclusion of the Yom Kippur service.

Let's have a closer look at the Shofar. Did you ever stop to think that it is one of the oldest wind instruments used by man? Only the reed-flute (called *Ugov* in the Bible) matches it in age (according to one opinion), but plays no part in our present day Divine service. The Shofar, however, is the same we used for thousands of years! All through the history of mankind new instruments have been invented and the old ones discarded, and only in the museums can we find an ancient flute or wind-pipe. Is it not remarkable that we should still cling to our age-old Shofar?

Of course, if you consider the Shofar as some "musical" instrument, you may not think much of it. It does not produce delicate and smooth tones as a modern bugle or trumpet or other wind instrument. But after all, to us the Shofar is not a "musical" instrument. It is not used for pleasure or entertainment. Far from it. It has a profound meaning. It is a call for repentance, heralding the Ten Days of Repentance, beginning with Rosh-Hashanah and culminating with Yom Kippur. Its message, in the words of the great Maimonides, is:

"Awake, ye sleepers, from your slumber, and ponder over your deeds; remember your Creator and go back to Him in penitence. Be not of those who miss realities in their pursuit of shadows, and waste their years in seeking after vain things which cannot profit or deliver. Look well to your souls and consider your acts; forsake each his evil ways and thoughts, and return to G-d so that He may have mercy upon you!"

Herein lies the most important function of the Shofar. The sounds of the Shofar are awe-inspiring, and touch off an unusual vibration in our heart, kindling a feeling of repentance, broken-heartedness and humility. Indeed, the very sounds of the Shofar, handed down to us by tradition, are very much like broken sobs and sighs. These sounds are three: *Tekiah* (the straight blast), *Shevarim* (three broken blasts) and *Teruah* (nine or more broken sounds). They are sounded in the following order:

1. *Tekiah—Shevarim-Teruah—Tekiah*
2. *Tekiah — Shevarim — Tekiah*
3. *Tekiah — Teruah — Tekiah*

In each case the sounds are repeated three times, making thirty sounds in all.

Altogether, no less than one hundred sounds of the Shofar are sounded in the course of the Rosh-Hashanah morning service (each of the above group of sounds is repeated three times, and in the same way three times during the service, making ninety sounds, and finally a single time again adding up to one hundred).

Rosh-Hashanah is called the Day of Sounding the Shofar. On this day it is imperative for every Jew to hear the Shofar.

Because the purpose of the Shofar is to inspire us with humility and repentance, we can well understand why the Shofar is not richly decorated. Decorations and ornaments do not make it unfit for use as long as they are on the outside only. But if they pierce the walls of the horn through and through, it becomes useless.

Perhaps this can serve us as a lesson on the importance of simplicity and humility. Like the Shofar which becomes unfit if the gold and silver of its ornaments cut through the bone of the Shofar, so we, too, become unfit human beings if we permit gold and silver to become so important in our lives as to "cut to the bone," and take possession of our minds and souls.

In days of old, the Shofar was used on very solemn occasions. We first find the name *Shofar* mentioned in connection with the Revelation on Mount Sinai, when "the voice of the Shofar was exceedingly strong, and all the people that were in the camp trembled." Thus, the Shofar we hear on Rosh-Hashanah ought to remind us of our acceptance of the Torah and our obligations under its laws.

The Shofar used to be sounded when war was waged upon a dangerous enemy. Thus, the Shofar we hear on Rosh-Hashanah ought to serve us as a battle cry to wage war against our inner enemy, our evil inclinations and passions.

The Shofar was sounded on the Jubilee Year, heralding freedom from slavery and want. The Shofar we hear on Rosh-Hashanah should likewise be the signal of our breaking the shackles of sin, so that we can start a new life with a pure heart attuned to the service of G-d and fellow man.

THE VOICE OF THE SHOFAR

To sound the Shofar on Rosh-Hashanah is a commandment in the Torah. It is a precept, like all other precepts of our faith. And like all other precepts, we have to make a blessing before fulfilling the commandment. The purpose of the blessing is to thank G-d for having made us holy through His commandments and for giving us an opportunity to do His will. The blessing is a preparation for us, so that we should not do these things in an absent-minded way, by force of habit only, but should know what we are about to do, and before whom we are going to do it, and the meaning of what we are going to do.

The blessing before the Shofar-blowing has the same purpose.

Now let us see what this blessing is:

"Blessed art Thou, O Lord our G-d, King of the Universe, who hath sanctified us (made us holy) by His commandments and commanded us *to hear the voice of the Shofar*."*

When you say in English "to hear," it means but one thing. But in Hebrew the same word (*lishmoa*, from the same root as *Shema*) means several things. It means, first of all, to *hear*, or to listen with our ears; it also means *to understand*, and finally it also means *to obey*.

And so when the *Baal Tokea* (the one who is about to sound the Shofar) makes the blessing for all of us, we are expected not only to *hear* the sound of the Shofar, but also to *understand* and *obey* its message.

What is the message of the Shofar?

---

* Note that we start the blessing in the *second* person — as though standing directly before G-d, but we finish it in the *third* person — for G-d is omnipresent and unseen, holy and quite beyond our understanding. All blessings have this form.

As already mentioned, the Shofar makes three sounds: *Tekiah*—the straight blast, like a long sigh; *Shevarim*—three broken sounds, like gasps; and *Teruah*—nine (or more) short sounds, like broken sobs or wails. Thus, the very sounds of the Shofar arouse and express our feelings: deep regret for any wrongs we may have committed in the past. But it is more than that; it is also a call to arms, like war drums. The Shofar tells us to take up arms against everything that does not let us fully practise our religion: against our passion; against our being lazy, negligent; against our being influenced by bad friends, and so on. It tells us: be brave, don't be afraid or lazy to fulfill all those holy precepts, such as praying every day, putting on Tefillin, wearing Tzitzith, observing the holy Sabbath, and so on. For our religious precepts and truths are worth fighting for.

And even if in the past we have not observed all these things very carefully, the Shofar tells us: It is not too late to start right now. G-d will forgive you for the past, if you will make a firm resolution to observe these things better in the future. This is the final message of the Shofar: the message of Divine forgiveness. That is why the final sound of the Shofar is a long blast, the *Tekiah gedolah* ("Great Tekiah"). This sound does not represent a sigh or a sob or a wail, but a cry of triumph, a shout of joy, for we are confident that G-d has accepted our repentance and has forgiven us. You may notice this expression of joy in the melody of the verses which are recited immediately after the *Tekioth*. For whereas the verses recited *before* the Tekioth are solemn and pleading, those recited *after* the Tekioth are jubiliant; they speak of happiness and joy, the kind of feeling that comes after sincere repentance.

And so this is the meaning of the blessing to hear (and to understand and to obey) the voice of the Shofar:

just as the word *lishmoa* has three meanings, so has the Shofar three chief messages: a call for repentance (to wake us from our indifference in the past); a call to arms (to overcome all obstacles in our way in the future); and finally—a message of G-d's mercy and forgiveness, so that we can start the new year with a clean slate, in a happy state of mind, like innocent children who have never sinned and have not an unhappy memory.

THE FIREMAN

(*A Parable*)

Many, many years ago, before there were any fire engines, and fire brigades, and electric fire alarms, and most houses were built of wood, a fire was a terrible thing. A whole town, or a good part of it, could go up in flames and smoke. And so, when fire broke out, everyone left his business or work, and rushed to help put out the fire. There used to be a watch tower which was taller than the other buildings, where a watchman kept a lookout all the time. As soon as he saw smoke or fire, he would sound the alarm. The townspeople would then form a human chain between the fire and the nearest well, and pass on to each other pails of water with which to put out the fire.

Once it happened that a lad from a small village came to town for the first time. He stopped at an inn, on the outskirts of the town. Suddenly he heard the sound of a bugle. He asked the innkeeper what it meant.

"Whenever we have a fire," the innkeeper explained to the lad, "we sound the bugle, and the fire is quickly put out."

"How wonderful!" thought the village lad. "What a surprise and sensation I will bring to my village!"

Thereupon, the village lad went and bought himself a bugle. When he returned to his village, he was full of excitement. He called all the villagers together. "Listen, good people," he exclaimed. "No need to be afraid of fire any more. Just watch me, and see how quickly I will put out a fire!"

Saying this, he ran to the nearest hut and set fire to its straw roof. The fire began to spread very quickly.

"Don't be alarmed!" cried the lad. "Now watch me."

The lad began to blow the bugle with all his might, interrupting it only to catch his breath, and to say, "Wait, this will put out the fire in no time!" But the fire did not seem to care much for the music, and merely hopped from one roof to another, until all the village was in flames.

The villagers now began to scold and curse the lad. "You fool," they cried. "Did you think that the mere blowing of the trumpet will put the fire out? It is only the call of an alarm, to wake up the people, if they are asleep, or to break them away from their business and work, and send them to the well to draw water and put out the fire!"

* * *

We are reminded of this story, when we think of the *Shofar* which is sounded many times on Rosh-Hashanah. Some people think, like that village lad, that the sound of the Shofar itself will do everything for them. They think that they may continue to "sleep," or go about their business, there being no need to change their way of life and daily conduct; the Shofar sounded in the synagogue will surely bring them a happy New Year.

But, like the bugle in the story, the Shofar is but the sound of an "alarm." It has a message: "Wake up, you sleepers, think about your ways, return to G-d, put out the 'fire' that is threatening to destroy your Jewish homes. Go to the Well, the Well of Living Waters, the Torah and Mitzvoth. Hurry, before it is too late!"

That is why, immediately after the Shofar is sounded, we exclaim: "Happy are the people who *understand* the meaning of the sound of the Shofar; they walk in Thy light, O G-d."

THE SHOFAR IN MIDRASH

The Shofar is made out of an animal horn. Any horn may be used for a Shofar, except the horn of a cow or a bull, for their horns are called in Hebrew "keren" and not "shofar," and also because their horn would be a reminder of the Golden Calf which the children of Israel had made in the desert, coming out of Egypt. It is hardly fitting to use such a reminder on the day of Rosh-Hashanah, when we pray for G-d's pleasure and benevolence.

Usually, and preferably, the Shofar is made out of a ram's horn, in memory of the ram which was offered instead of Isaac, who had allowed himself to be bound and placed on the altar as a sacrifice to G-d.

Rabbi Abuhu said, Why do we use a Shofar made of a ram's horn for our Rosh-Hashanah Tekioth? (In memory of the Ram of Isaac), for G-d said, Sound the Tekioth unto Me through a Shofar made of a ram's horn, and I will remember the binding of Isaac and think of you as though you, too, were ready to offer your lives unto Me.

* * *

In the portion of the Torah about the Binding of Isaac, which we read on the second day of Rosh-Hashanah, it is written (Gen. 22:13), "And Abraham lifted up his eyes, and looked, and behold a ram caught afterwards in the thicket by his horns." Abraham saw the ram caught in one thicket after another.

Said Rav Huna the son of Rav Yitzchak, The ram caught again and again in the thick bushes showed Abraham that his children would be caught in one exile after another, but in the end they will be redeemed by the sound of the ram's horn. (*Midrash Rabba, Vayyikra* 29).

Rabbi Chanina ben Dossa said, every part of that ram had its importance: the ashes of the ram were the foundation of the inner altar in the Beth Hamikdosh; the ten tendons of the ram made up the strings of King David's harp; the skin of the ram made up Elijah's leather girdle; and of the two horns—the left one was sounded at Mount Sinai, when the Torah was given, and the right one, the larger one, will be sounded when the Jewish exiles will be gathered from all corners of the earth, as it is written (*Isaiah* 27), "And it shall come to pass on that day that the great Shofar will be sounded . . ." (*Pirkei Rabbi Eliezer* 31).

* * *

The Shofar has to be bent, to show that we have to bend our hearts to our Heavenly Father.

* * *

The Shofar must not be decorated either by gold, or even by painting anything on it. If one made a golden mouthpiece to the Shofar it can no longer serve as a Shofar. The only thing permitted is some carvings on the horn itself, without adding anything to it.

* * *

One must listen to the sound of the Shofar itself, and not to the echo of it. If one hears just an echo of the Tekioth, he has not observed the Mitzvah of Shofar. This law was important to the Jews in the time of the Inquisition in Spain, when the *Marranos* (Jews in secret) used to go out into the woods, hills and caves to sound the Shofar, for if they were caught at it, they would be burnt alive at the stake.

Similarly, in certain Arab countries the Jews were not allowed to sound the Shofar, for it used to frighten the Arabs, who knew that the Jewish Redeemer would some day come with the sound of the Shofar.

* * *

The Shofar is sounded on Rosh-Hashanah after the reading of the Torah, before (as well as during) *Musaph.* Although a Mitzvah should not be delayed, and the Shofar should have been sounded at the beginning of the service, there was a good reason for delaying the Shofar until after the reading of the Torah. For it happened, in a certain Jewish community surrounded by enemies, that the Shofar was sounded in the early morning. The enemies thought that the Jews were calling for a rebellion to fight against them, so they surrounded them and killed them. It was then decided to sound the Shofar after the reading of the Torah. For, when the enemies saw that the Jews had already said part of their prayer peacefully, had read the Shema, said the Amidah, and read in the Torah, they realized that this was a peaceful gathering for prayer, and not for rebellion against them. (*Talmud Jerushalmi, Rosh Hashanah,* 4:5).

Rashi explains that there was a time when the Jews were forbidden to sound the Shofar. Guards were posted to watch them until the *Shacharith* service was concluded. The Jews therefore sounded the Shofar later, during the *Musaph service,* and the rule thus remained for sounding the Shofar *after* the Shacharith service. There is also another reason: for by then the worshippers are already crowned with Mitzvoth: Tzitzith, Shema, and reading of the Torah; then comes the Shofar and brings them forgiveness.

THE PARDON

(*A Parable*)

A king went a-hunting in the forest. Chasing after a deer, he went deep into the woods, and when he looked around, he found himself alone. He began to look for a way out of the woods, and for the road which would lead him back to his city and palace.

In his search he met some country folk, but nobody recognized him, or wanted to have anything to do with him. When he began to speak to them, they did not even understand what he was saying, nor did they care.

Wandering about in the woods for a long time, the king heard a fine melody which someone was playing on a flute. Following the sound, the king came across a man and engaged him in conversation. The man recognized the king at once, and spoke to him with humility and respect. The king saw that here was a man after his heart, and liked him at once. When he told the man that he was hoping to meet someone who would be able to lead him out of the woods and back to his palace and throne, the man was happy to do it, and the king felt grateful to him. He invited him to his palace and gave him a place of honor among his royal counsellors and advisers. Then he ordered costly garments for his friend, befitting his rank.

Some time later, the king's friend disobeyed the king. The king became very angry, and ordered him to appear before the royal court for trial.

When the day of trial came, the king's friend took off his robes, and put on the simple clothes he wore on the day when he first met the king. He also took his flute with him, and appeared before the royal court very humble and repentant.

Before passing judgment the king asked him if he had any request to make.

"Permit me, Your Majesty, to play a melody on my flute," the defendant asked, and his request was granted.

He played the beautiful melody which he had played on that day when he had met the king for the first time.

The king remembered it well. At once that happy meeting came to his mind, when the stranger had made the king so happy, and led him out of the forest back to his palace. The king thereupon pardoned his friend and took him back into his grace and favor.

* * *

This story will help us understand a little better the meaning of the blowing of the Shofar. For what happened to us is very similar to the story.

When G-d was about to give the Torah, he turned to various peoples, but no people on earth wanted to accept it. In the end G-d turned to our people, and we accepted Him and the Torah with the beautiful words of "Naase v'nishma"—We will Do and Obey—a promise to fulfill G-d's commands without question. We took upon ourselves the Divine rule, and proclaimed G-d as the King of the whole world. This pleased G-d very much.

When Rosh-Hashanah comes, and all our actions come before G-d and are weighed on the scale, the good deeds against the bad deeds during the whole year, we may rightly be worried what the outcome may be, if we were judged according to our merits. We want G-d to be merciful to us and forgive us no matter what our record may have been in the past. Therefore we appear before G-d in the way we appeared before Him on that great day at Sinai. On that day the sound of the Shofar was heard, and we sang the beautiful melody of "Naase v'nishma." Then G-d remembers that day and turns towards us with mercy and forgiveness, and our love for G-d and G-d's love for us becomes as strong as ever. Then we may be sure that we will be inscribed unto a New Year of good health and happiness.

THE CALL OF THE SHOFAR

(A Story)

1.

Once upon a time there lived a poor orphan, who had neither father nor mother. His name was Moshe, but because he was a small boy and an orphan everybody called him "Moshele." As long as he was still a little boy he went to "Cheder" where he learned "Chumash" and "Gemarah" together with the other children, but when he grew a little older he had to go out and earn his livelihood. So a collection was made to provide him with a basketful of merchandise, such as needles, buttons and other trinkets, and Moshele set out to sell them to the peasants and farmers in the villages and hamlets that surrounded his native town.

It was a very hard job, of course. In the summer the heat was unbearable, and in the winter the snow and icy winds often made his teeth chatter. But Moshele did not mind. His only regret was that he could not go to the Yeshivah, for he wanted to become a scholar.

One wintry day Moshele was trudging along on the snow-covered road, with his basketful of merchandise under his arm. He knew some Psalms by heart and he recited them cheerily as he walked. Snow kept on falling from the grey skies, and soon he found himself plodding ankle deep in snow. It was getting difficult to walk, and it was even more difficult to follow the road which was now completely covered with snow as far as the eye could see. Unwittingly he strayed off the road and presently found himself in a little wood. Moshele felt very tired and decided to have a little rest. He noticed a big stump and sat down on it, placing his basket down on the snow. "No, you must not fall asleep," he kept on telling himself, "it is very dangerous; you might freeze to death!" So he sat there huddled up and shivering, trying in vain to keep himself warm, and his eyes open.

Suddenly he felt a breath of warmth through his body. He found himself sitting by a nice, cosy fire, and stretched out his hands and feet towards it. He felt as if sharp needles were pricking his finger tips, but that stopped soon as the flames blazed bigger and bigger. . . .

2.

A peasant passing on the road in his sledge noticed the huddled figure of a lad almost fully covered with snow. He stopped his horse and ran to the body. Brushing the snow off, he found that the body was almost frozen stiff, with no sign of life.

Without losing time, the peasant set to work. He pulled out his knife and cut up the clothing around the still body. Then he started to rub it briskly with snow. After half an hour's work the blood began to flow in the young body again, and the boy stirred. The peasant then carried the lad to his sledge, covered him up, and drove his horse as fast as he could to his home in the nearby village. There he again rubbed the body of the lad with snow, until his skin began to glow, and finally poured some hot brandy down the lad's throat. Moshele opened his eyes and closed them again. Thereupon the peasant carried him onto the oven and covered him up snugly. Moshele fell asleep.

The crowing of the cock woke him up very early next morning. Moshele opened his eyes and looked around. He could not understand where he was, and why so many pins and needles were pricking him all over his body.

The farmer's wife was up and came up to see him. "How do you feel?" she asked him in Russian, for she was a Russian peasant-woman. "Alright," Moshele said, still wondering what had happened to him.

The woman boiled up some tea for him, and he drank it gratefully.

"What is your name?" she asked him.

Moshele tried to think hard, but could not remember. "I don't know," he said, thinking how strange it was that he could not remember his own name.

"Never mind," said the peasant woman, "we'll call you Peter."

3.

Thus Moshele, or Peter as he was now called by all, remained in the peasant's home, little knowing that he was a Jewish boy and did not belong there at all.

When summer came, Peter helped the farmer in all the work in the field: ploughing, sowing and reaping. Peter was an industrious, capable lad, and the farmer was very pleased with him.

The summer passed by and autumn came. One day the farmer said to Peter: "To-morrow we shall drive to town and take some of our products to the market."

Peter was very glad, and looked forward to seeing the town. When they finally got there the next day, the market place and all the streets were deserted. When they passed by the synagogue, they saw it was crowded with worshippers, and the peasant realized that it was a Jewish holiday. There was nothing to do but to drive back home. But Peter was fascinated by the quaint synagogue and begged the peasant to stay in town a while. "Very good then," said the peasant, "you will meet me in the public house," and he went to have a drink, while Peter felt an irresistable desire to look into the synagogue.

Peter came in quietly and stood by the door. The

worshippers wrapped in praying-shawls seemed very intent on their prayers; many of them were weeping. No one paid any attention to him. Peter looked closely around him. His heart began to beat faster. Somehow the scene was familiar to him. Had he ever been here before? Slowly his memory returned to him, as everything in the synagogue brought new memories into his conscience. The tune and melodies of the cantor were familiar to him. The scrolls of the Torah that had just been brought out of the Ark were familiar too. As if glued to his place, Peter stood motionless and stared. . . .

Peter did not know how long he stood there, but presently he noticed a little excitement among the worshippers. The very air appeared to become tense with sacred animation, as if angels were fluttering in the air. Peter was transfixed with awe.

The silence was broken by the shaking voice of the aged cantor, and immediately the entire community joined in fervent prayer. For some time the roar of the whole community praying seemed to shake the very walls of the synagogue, and then it began to subside gradually, until a solemn silence fell again. In the stillness of the air the sobbing of the cantor became clearly audible, and Peter found himself weeping too.

Suddenly he heard "Tekiah-ah-ah" and the blast of the ram's horn pierced the air.

"Shevari-i-m Teruah," and again the broken sound of the Shofar seemed to stab Peter's heart. "Tekiah-ah-ah," the Shofar called again. . . .

"Moshele, you are a Jew," the Shofar called. "Moshele, you are a Jew! Hurry now . . . Now is the time to return to G-d . . . Tekiah-ah . . . Teruah-ah-ah. . . .

Everything now became very clear to Moshele. . . .

"O dear G-d, forgive me," Moshele cried, and fainted.

SHOFAR ON THE HIGH SEAS

A great and saintly Rabbi was once aboard ship, together with two of his disciples. Rosh-Hashanah drew near and land was not in sight yet. So the Rabbi and his disciples prepared to spend the Holy Days of Rosh-Hashanah on the High Seas.

On the night of Rosh-Hashanah a terrific storm broke out. The ship was tossed about by the huge waves and was in grave danger of breaking up. The big waves swept over the ship again and again, flooding it from bow to stern. The sailors worked hard to bale the water out, until they had no strength left in them. It seemed only a matter of time before the ship would sink, unless the storm passed immediately.

During all this time the saintly Rabbi sat in his cabin, engrossed in prayer, paying no attention to the storm threatening the ship. At dawn, when the storm had not let up, his two disciples decided to tell the Rabbi of the danger that threatened all of them. Entering his cabin, and finding him engrossed in prayer, they hesitated and withdrew, finding no courage to disturb him. A little while later they tried again, but again they turned back, not daring to disturb him. Finally, when the storm seemed to have reached its height and it was a matter of minutes before they would all be drowned, the disciples decided there was no time to be lost. With trembling voices and tears in their eyes they approached the Rabbi and told him of the danger they were in.

"If this is the case, then waste no time. Bring the Shofar quickly and let us fulfill the sacred commandment of sounding the Shofar while we still are alive," the Rabbi said.

The disciples brought the Shofar, and soon the sound of the Shofar was heard through the boat — "Tekiah,

Shevarim, Teruah, Tekiah . . . ah . . . ah . . ." And the high winds seemed to snatch up the sounds of the Shofar and carry them far away. . . ."

Suddenly the wind began to calm down, as if afraid to drown out the holy sounds of the Shofar. Also, the roar of the sea grew quieter and quieter, and before long there was perfect calm over the water. The last sounds of the Shofar rang clearly in the stillness of the early morning.

It was a wonderful miracle!

The captain and the sailors and many passengers, following the sound of the Shofar, came to the Rabbi's cabin, where they found the Rabbi and his two disciples joyfully concluding the solemn Shofar service.

Amazed and full of awe, they bowed their heads in respect, and when the Rabbi concluded the service, the captain said, "That is certainly a magical horn that you have there, for it has changed the stormy sea into a calm lake. If you will sell it to me, I will give you anything you wish for it."

The Rabbi smiled as he answered: "No, my friend, it is not a magical horn, but a *Shofar,* a simple ram's horn, which we Jews are commanded to sound on the solemn days of our New Year. It raises a storm in our hearts, which is mightier than the storm of the sea, for it calls us to return to G-d with humility.

"I did not know," the Rabbi continued, "that it would save us all. All I wanted to do was to fulfill one more Divine commandment in the last moments of life left to us. But G-d is merciful, and spared us all, so that we might live a good and holy life. Let us show our gratitude to G-d by obeying His commandments always, in times of safety as well as in times of danger, for we are always at His mercy."

RABBI AMNON

1.

More than eight hundred years ago there lived a very great man in the city of Maintz. His name was Rabbi Amnon. Rabbi Amnon was a great scholar and a very pious man. He was loved and respected by Jews and non-Jews alike, and his name was known far and wide. Even the Duke of Hessen, the ruler of the land, admired and respected Rabbi Amnon for his wisdom, scholarship and piety. Many a time the Duke invited him to his palace and consulted him on all matters of State.

Rabbi Amnon never accepted any reward for his services to the Duke or to the State. From time to time, however, Rabbi Amnon would ask the Duke to ease the position of the Jews in his land, to abolish some of the decrees and restrictions which existed against the Jews at that time, and generally to enable them to live in peace and security. This was the only favor that Rabbi Amnon ever requested from the Duke, and the Duke never turned down his request. Thus Rabbi Amnon and his brethren lived happily for many years.

2.

Now, the other statesmen of the Duke grew envious of Rabbi Amnon. Most envious of them all was the Duke's secretary, who could not bear to see the honor and respect which Rabbi Amnon enjoyed from his master, which was rapidly developing into a great friendship between the Duke and the Rabbi. The secretary began to seek ways and means to discredit Rabbi Amnon in the eyes of the Duke.

One day the secretary said to the Duke:

"Sire, why should you not persuade Rabbi Amnon to

become a Christian, like ourselves? I am sure that considering the honor and many favors he has enjoyed at your generous hand, he will gladly abandon his faith and accept ours."

The Duke thought it was not a bad idea. When Rabbi Amnon came to his palace the next day, he said to him:

"My good friend, Rabbi Amnon, I know you have been loyal and devoted to me for many years. Now I wish to ask you a personal favor. Abandon your faith, and become a good Christian like myself. If you do, I shall make you the greatest man in the whole of my State; you shall have honor and riches like no other man, and next to me you shall be the most powerful man in my State. . . ."

Rabbi Amnon grew very pale. For a moment he could find no words to reply to he Duke, but after a while he said:

"O illustrious Monarch! For many years I have served you faithfully, and my being a Jew in no way lessened my loyalty to you or to the State. On the contrary, my faith bids me to be loyal and faithful to the land of my sojourn. I am ready and willing to sacrifice everything I possess, even my very life, for you as well as for the State. There is one thing, however, that I can never part with—that is my faith. I am bound by an unbreakable covenant to my faith, the faith of my forefathers. Do you want me to betray my people, my G-d? Would you want a man to serve you that has no respect for his religion, for the bonds and ties he holds most sacred? If I betray my G-d, could you ever trust me never to betray you? Surely, the Duke cannot mean it. The Duke is jesting!"

"No, no . . ." the Duke said, though he sounded a little uncertain, for inwardly the Duke was impressed with Rabbi Amnon's reply. Rabbi Amnon hoped that the matter was settled, but when he arrived at the palace the next day, the Duke repeated his request. Rabbi Amnon became very unhappy, and began to avoid visiting the palace, unless it was absolutely necessary.

One day the Duke, impatient at Rabbi Amnon's obstinacy, put it very bluntly to him: He must either become a Christian at once or take the consequences.

Pressed to give his answer immediately, Rabbi Amnon finally begged the Duke to allow him three days in which to consider the matter. This the Duke granted him.

3.

No sooner did Rabbi Amnon leave the Duke, than he realized his grave sin. "Dear G-d," he thought, "what have I done? Am I lacking in faith and courage that I requested three days for consideration? Can there be any but one answer? How could I show such weakness even for one moment?! O gracious G-d, forgive me. . . ."

Rabbi Amnon arrived home broken-hearted. He secluded himself in his room and spent the next three days in prayer and supplication, begging G-d's forgiveness for the weakness of heart he had shown even for one moment.

When Rabbi Amnon did not arrive at the palace on the third day, the Duke became very angry, and ordered his men to bring Rabbi Amnon in chains.

The Duke hardly recognized Rabbi Amnon, so much had the venerable man changed in the course of the last three days. However, the Duke quickly brushed aside whatever feeling of sympathy he might have felt for his erstwhile friend, and said to him sternly:

"How dare you disregard my command! Why did you not appear before me in time to give me your answer? For your sake I trust you have decided to do as I tell you. It will be bad for you otherwise. . . ."

Although Rabbi Amnon was now a broken man physically, his spirit was stronger than ever.

"Sire," Rabbi Amnon answered him fearlessly, "there can be but one answer: I shall remain a loyal Jew as long as I breathe!"

The Duke was beside himself with wrath. "It is now more than the question of your becoming a Christian. You have disobeyed me by not coming voluntarily to give me your answer. For this you must be punished. . . ."

"Sire," Rabbi Amnon said, "by requesting three days for consideration I have sinned gravely against my G-d."

These brave words enraged the Duke even more. "For sinning against your G-d," the Duke said angrily, "let Him avenge Himself. I shall punish you for disobeying MY orders. Your legs sinned against me, for they refused to come to me; therefore your legs shall be cut off!"

4.

With very faint signs of life the legless body of Rabbi Amnon was sent back to his home, to his grief stricken family. It was the day before Rosh-Hashanah.

The news about Rabbi Amnon's dreadful fate spread throughout the whole city. Every one was horrified and distressed. It was a very tragic Day of Judgment for the Jews of Maintz, who assembled in *shul* the following morning.

Despite his terrible suffering Rabbi Amnon remembered that it was Rosh-Hashanah, and he requested to be taken to *shul*. At his request he was placed in front of the holy Ark.

All the worshippers, men, women and children wept terribly seeing their beloved Rabbi in such agony, and never were any more heart-rending prayers offered than on that day of Rosh-Hashanah.

When the "chazan" began to recite the Musaph prayer, Rabbi Amnon motioned that there be made an interval while he offered a special prayer to G-d. Silence fell upon all the worshippers, and Rabbi Amnon began to say "Unesaneh toikef." The congregation repeated every word and their hearts went out to G-d in prayer. Then they most solemnly recited the prayer of "Oleinu," and when the words "He is our G-d, and no other" were reached, Rabbi Amnon cried them out with his last remaining strength, and passed away.

* * *

The prayer "Unesaneh Toikef"—the most solemn prayer of Rosh-Hashanah and Yom Kippur, is recited in every Jewish community in the world, and the courage of Rabbi Amnon, the undying author of this prayer, serves as an inspiration to all of us.

TASHLICH

In his explanation of our customs and tradition, the Maharil* traces back the custom of *Tashlich* on Rosh-Hashanah to very ancient times. It is performed shortly before sunset on the afternoon of the first day of Rosh-Hashanah (unless it falls on Shabbos, then on the second), by going to the banks of a river, lake, or any stretch of water, where certain prayers are recited followed by the symbolic shaking of the corners of our garments.

The three last verses of the prophet Micah, which we say at Tashlich, contain the explanation for this custom. We say: "Who is a G-d like unto Thee, pardoning iniquity and forgiving transgression to the residue of His

* Rabbi Jacòb ben Moses Halevi, famous Talmudist and authority on Jewish law and custom; d. Worms, Germany, 5187 (1427).

heritage. He retaineth not His anger for ever, because He delighteth in kindness. He will again have mercy on us. He will suppress our iniquities; yes, *Thou wilt cast our sins into the depth of the sea.*" The Maharil gives us a further explanation of Tashlich. The Midrash tells us that when Abraham and Isaac went to Mount Moriah for the Akedah, they had to cross a river, one of the forms which Satan adopted to prevent them from fulfilling G-d's command. The floods threatened to swallow them, but Abraham prayed "Save us, O G-d, for the water has reached our very lives," and they were saved from the floods. Thus, says the Maharil, no obstacle should keep us back from fulfilling any command of G-d. He who can show the selfless love of Abraham and his readiness to die for the Divine word, can be sure that "his sins will be cast into the sea."

The Tashlich prayer, recited at the banks of a river, lake, or sea, where there is fish, has another significance in arousing in us thoughts of repentance. For it reminds us of the insecurity of fish-life, and the danger of fish to fall for bait, or be caught in the fisherman's net. Our life, too, is full of pitfalls and temptations.

We are reminded of the classical parable of Rabbi Akiba, who defied the decree prohibiting the study of the Torah which the Roman Emperor Hadrian tried to impose on the Jews. Asked why he risked his life by studying and spreading the teachings of the Torah, Rabbi Akiba replied by means of the following parable:

A hungry fox came to the bank of a stream. He saw the fish swimming restlessly in the water. Said the sly fox to the fish: "I see you are living in mortal fear lest you fall into the fisherman's net. Come out onto the dry bank, and you will escape the fisherman's net, and we'll live happily together, as my ancestors lived with yours." But the fish scoffed at the cunning fox, and replied: "If in the water, which is our very life, we are in danger, surely our leaving the water would mean certain death to us!"

The Torah is our very life, and we cannot live without it any more than fish can live without water. Could we save ourselves by abandoning our way of life, the way of the Torah?

Such are the reflections which *Tashlich* arouses in the heart of the worshipper.

Finally, the fish serve as a further reminder of the "ever watchful eye" of Providence, for fish have no eyelids; their eyes are always open. So nothing can be hidden from G-d. By the same token, one derives courage and hope through faith in G-d, for the Guardian of Israel never sleeps nor slumbers.

In the Middle Ages the custom of Tashlich was used several times to accuse the Jews of casting a spell over the water, or even poisoning it, and the Rabbis were, on occasion, obliged to prohibit the observance of Tashlich by their communities in those days, so as not to endanger their lives.

Rabbi Abahu said, The Ministering Angels asked the Holy One, Blessed is He: Master of the Universe, why do not the Jews recite song (Hallel) before Thee on Rosh-Hashanah and Yom Kippur?

Replied G-d to them: When a king sits on the Throne of Judgment, with the Book of Life and Death opened before Him, is it right that the Jews should sing unto Me at this time?

(*Talmud Babli*, Archin 10a)

THE DAYS OF REPENTANCE

THE STORY OF GEDALIAH

(A chapter from our ancient past)

1.

NEBUCHADNEZZAR, king of Babylon had accomplished his purpose. He had completely subdued the Kingdom of Judah, destroyed its capital Jerusalem, and its most sacred shrine, the Beth Hamikdosh. He had slain or captured most of the royal family and the nobility of the land. The upper classes of the Jewish people, including the leaders of the priesthood and the chief civil and military officers, were led captives *en masse* to Babylon. Many of them were mercilessly put to death at Riblah. Judah was crushed and bereaved of its best sons.

However, Nebuchadnezzar did not wish to turn the land of Judah into a complete desert. He permitted the poorer classes to remain in Judah to till the soil and to tend their vineyards. Over them Nebuchadnezzar had appointed Gedaliah, the son of Ahikam, as governor.

The prophet Jeremiah had been allowed to choose between remaining in Judah and going to Babylon as an honored guest of the Babylonian royal house. He chose to remain with his brethren on the holy soil. Jeremiah went to Mizpah, a short way north of Jerusalem, where Gedaliah had established the seat of his governorship, and offered him his fullest support. Gedaliah gratefully accepted, and Mizpah now became also the spiritual center of the people.

Gedaliah was a wise man, gentle and modest. He zealously began to encourage the people to cultivate the fields and vineyards, and thus lay the foundation of security. Under the wise administration of Gedaliah, the Jewish community began to prosper. Its fame began to spread abroad. Many Jews who had fled to places of safety in neighboring lands during the war of destruction, were attracted by the news of the revival of the Jewish community in Judah. They came to Gedaliah in Mizpah and were warmly welcomed by him. The Jewish Governor exhorted his brethren to remain loyal to the king of Babylon and promised them peace and security. His advice was well taken. The Babylonian garrison stationed in the land did not molest them; on the contrary, offered them protection against unfriendly neighbors. The young Jewish commonwealth was well on its way to recovery when it was suddenly struck by a cowardly deed of treachery and bloodshed.

2.

Among the refugees who had joined Gedaliah in Mizpah was Ishmael, the son of Nathaniah, a descendant of the royal house of Zedekiah, the last king of Judah. Ishmael was an ambitious man who would stop at nothing to attain his goal. The honor and success which Gedaliah had won filled him with cruel jealousy. Ishmael began to plot against Gedaliah. He found an ally in the king of Ammon, who had been following with apprehension the growth of the new Jewish colony.

The conspiracy became known to Johanan, the son of Koreah, a devoted officer of Gedaliah. Johanan warned the governor of the danger threatening his person. Gedaliah, however, being of a true and generous nature, shrank from believing such treachery. When Johanan offered to slay Ishmael secretly before the latter could carry out his evil plans, Gedaliah indignantly rejected the proposal.

In the meantime, Ishmael bided his time. Before

long the opportunity he was waiting for presented itself. He was invited by the governor to a feast at Mizpah on New Year's day. Ishmael arrived at the banquet in the company of ten followers. During the feast, the ruthless band attacked and slew the governor. Having assassinated their host, they commenced a terrible massacre. Ishmael murdered many prominent followers of Gedaliah, and put to the sword the small Chaldean garrison stationed at Mizpah. His murderous deed accomplished, Ishmael left Mizpah with many captives, heading for Ammon.

Johanan and a few of his brave men had escaped the massacre, for they were not in Mizpah at that time. When Johanan learned of the terrible tragedy, he rallied additional help and pursued the assassin. Overtaking Ishmael near Gibeon in Benjamin, Johanan succeeded in freeing the captives, but Ishmael with a few followers managed to escape to the land of Ammon.

3.

The plight of the Jews was now sad indeed. The assassination of Gedaliah and of the Babylonian garrison would draw the wrath of Nebuchadnezzar upon the remnants of the people in Judah. They were sorely afraid of his punishment. Yet whither could they turn? The only haven of refuge seemed to be Egypt, where the hand of Nebuchadnezzar had not reached yet. But that country was hateful to them. Although some nine hundred years had passed since their ancestors had been liberated from Egypt after centuries of slavery, Egypt was still regarded with aversion. Their despair and fright was so great, however, that the poor people did decide to seek escape in Egypt, and set out on their way southward.

The hard-pressed Jews halted in Beth-Lehem and turned to Jeremiah for advice. The faithful prophet who had shared in all their trials and misfortunes and had clung to them with unwavering affection, was still among them. To him they now turned their anxious eyes, promising to abide by whatever counsel he might give them.

For ten days Jeremiah prayed to G-d, and finally he received a Divine message which he immediately told to the assembled people:

> "Thus says the G-d of Israel . . . if you will still dwell in this land, I will build you, and not destroy you, and I will plant you, and not pluck you up . . . Fear not the king of Babylon, of whom you are afraid . . . for I am with you to save you . . . But if you say, 'We will not dwell in this land,' disobeying the voice of your G-d, saying, 'No, but we will go into the land of Egypt,' . . . then it shall come to pass that the sword which you feared shall overtake you there in the land of Egypt, and the famine whereof you were afraid shall follow close after you in Egypt; and there you shall die . . . G-d hath spoken to you, O remnant of Judah, go not to Egypt; know you with certainty, for I have warned you this day!"

But Jeremiah's words fell on deaf ears. The people had already formed their resolution, and had only hoped that the prophet would confirm it. In spite of their solemn pledge to Jeremiah that they would follow his advice, they accused the prophet of plotting together with his disciple Baruch, the son of Neriah, to deliver them into the hands of the Chaldeans. Then they all proceeded on their way to Egypt, forcing Jeremiah and Baruch to accompany them.

When the refugees reached the border of Egypt, they halted. Here Jeremiah once again warned his brethren that the safety they sought in Egypt would be short-lived. He predicted that before long Egypt would be conquered by Nebuchadnezzar and destroyed. The prophet further warned them of the dangers besetting them in mixing with the idolatrous Egyptians. If they should return to idolatry, which had been the cause of all their misfortunes in the past, they would seal their fate beyond hope.

Unfortunately, the prophet's warnings and entreaties were in vain. The Jewish refugees settled in Egypt and before long abandoned their faith in G-d. They sank to the level of the heathen practices of the Egyptians.

A few years later there was a political upheaval in Egypt when Pharaoh Hophra was assassinated. Nebuchadnezzar took advantage of the situation. He invaded and destroyed the land, and most of the Jewish refugees perished in this invasion and war. Thus Jeremiah's dreadful prophecy came true again.

Where and when the aged prophet died is not known with certainty. It is believed that he and his faithful disciple Baruch spent their last years with their exiled brethren in Babylon.

In memory of the assassination of Gedaliah and the tragedy that it brought upon our brethren in those days, so soon after the Destruction of the Beth Hamikdosh, we fast on the 3rd day of Tishrei, the *Fast of Gedaliah.*

READINGS FROM THE TORAH ON THE FAST OF GEDALIAH

The Fast of Gedaliah is one of four Fast Days connected with the Destruction of the Beth-Hamikdosh. As on other fasts, the portion read in the morning and in the afternoon (at Minchah) is that of *Vayehal* (Ex. 32:11-14; 34:1-10). Three men are called up for the reading, and at Minchah, the third is also *Maftir* (Isaiah 55:6-56:8).

The portion contains the moving prayer of Moses, after the children of Israel had made the Golden Calf. It contains the Thirteen Divine Attributes of mercy and forgiveness, which G-d proclaimed at that time, and which are invoked in prayers of forgiveness (such as *Tachanun, Selichoth,* etc.).

The message of this portion is that no matter how great the transgression — and could there be a greater one than that of the Golden Calf so soon after the Revelation at Sinai? — G-d is always ready to forgive the sincerely repentant sinner. That "it is human to err and Divine to forgive" is a lesson frequently found in the Torah and in the books of the Prophets. Sin may be excused and forgiven, but *persistence* in sin is unforgivable. Yet sincere repentance never remains unanswered.

The same message is emphasized in the Haphtorah read at Minchah—"Seek G-d when He may be found, call unto Him, when He is near. Let the wicked man forsake his way and the sinful man his thoughts, and return to G-d, that He may be compassionate unto him, and to our G-d who forgives abundantly." Lest the sinner think that he is beyond forgiveness, having failed so often, the prophet continues, "For My thoughts are not like your thoughts, and your ways are not My ways, says G-d." For as G-d is Infinite, so is His forgiveness.

RABBI SAADIAH AND THE INNKEEPER

Came the month of Elul, followed by the Days of Repentance, and the famous Rabbi Saadiah Gaon would set aside his books of the Talmud and his writings for many hours each day, which he would spend in prayer and repentance. He prayed more fervently than ever, with a broken heart and with tears in his eyes, as if he were the greatest sinner on earth.

His disciples, who knew what a saintly man he was, could not understand what came over their master. Finally they asked him about it, and this is what he told them:

"Do not suspect me of having broken a law of the Torah, G-d forbid," Rabbi Saadiah began. "Nevertheless, I have good reason to repent and pray to G-d for forgiveness. I learnt this from an ordinary Jewish innkeeper.

"Once, during my travels, I stayed at a Jewish inn. The innkeeper did not know me, and treated me as kindly as he would treat any Jewish wayfarer. Before long, however, I was recognized in the town. The news of my arrival spread throughout the community and the whole community gathered to welcome me.

"When the innkeeper found out who his guest was, he began to honor me and serve me with awe and humility, and to do all he could to please me. At last, when I was leaving, all the people gathered to bid me farewell. The innkeeper then pushed his way through the crowd, fell at my feet, and implored me with tears in his eyes to forgive him. 'But you did all you could for me and more than enough!' I exclaimed, and the heartbroken innkeeper replied, 'I implore you, Rabbi, to forgive me for those days when I had not known of your greatness, and did not serve you as well as I know now.'

"Now, my friends," concluded Rabbi Saadiah, with tears streaming down his saintly face, "think carefully about it. If a man can be so humble when it comes to honoring another man, made of flesh and blood, how careful must we be in the way we honor, love, and serve our Creator!

"The closer we come to G-d, the more we understand His greatness, and the more we must feel repentant for our behavior in the past, no matter how hard we tried. Every day I learn more and more about G-d, and every day I feel ashamed because yesterday, when I did not know as much, my love for G-d and my devotion to Him were not as strong as today; and tomorrow, I know, I shall feel this way, too, about today."

MAIMONIDES ON TESHUVAH

The great Maimonides, Rabbi Moshe ben Maimon, Talmudist, codifier, philosopher and physician, who flourished some 800 years ago, wrote a special section on *Teshuvah* ("Hilechoth Teshuvah"—the Laws of Repentance) in his great work, "Mishneh Torah."

In chapter 4 of this section, Maimonides enumerates twenty-four types of transgressions which should be especially avoided, inasmuch as it is very difficult to repent of them.

The difficulty consists in the fact that these transgressions are either very serious, or, conversely, seem very light in the eyes of the transgressor, so that he may feel that no repentance is possible in the first case, or necessary in the second; or, again, they are of such a nature that to make amends for them and correct them is indeed almost impossible.

Of the twenty four kinds of transgression, Maimonides states, four types are so grievous that G-d withholds His special grace from the transgressor, though in other cases G-d helps the would-be repenter to carry out his good intentions of returning to G-d. These four types of transgression are:

(1) He who is instrumental in causing people to sin, or in preventing them from doing a Mitzvah.

(2) He who uses his influence to mislead someone from the path of the Torah.

(3) One who permits his own child to stray from the path of the Torah, failing to give him the proper education and guidance; or one who has an opportunity to prevent someone from committing a sin, and does not do it.

(4) He who deludes himself by thinking, "I will

sin now, and repent later," or that "the Day of Atonement will wipe my sins off, anyway."

The next five types of transgression are such that by the sinner's own attitude and actions he blocks his road to Teshuvah. They are:

(5) One who separates himself from the congregation, and does not participate in the Jewish communal life and institutions, thus depriving himself of the merits that belong to the entire congregation, and of the merits of congregational prayer and repentance.

(6) He who denies the words of the Sages and scorns their holy writings, thus depriving himself of the great spiritual benefits which they contain, with their influence and inspiration.

(7) One who scoffs at the Divine commandments, for he will not likely repent of his sins.

(8) One who despises his spiritual teachers, for without such guidance he will not likely find his way to repentance.

(9) He who dislikes words of rebuke, for it is very difficult for a person to attain Teshuvah without outside influence.

The next class of five types of transgression, Maimonides says, consist of transgressions for which it is difficult to make amends or restitution. They are:

(10) When one commits an offense against, or causes a loss to, an entire congregation (as in the case of misusing public funds), for it is impossible for the offender to obtain forgiveness from each and every individual of the congregation wronged by his action.

(11) When one shares in a theft committed by another person, not knowing the owner of the thing stolen,

and thus being unable to make restitution. Besides, by sharing in the theft, he encourages the thief to steal, and thus he is guilty of a sin which is difficult to correct.

(12) Finding something in the street, and failing to seek the owner of the lost thing immediately; thus, it will probably be impossible for him to trace the rightful owner of the thing later, and he will remain in possession of something not belonging to him.

(13) Offending a passing poor man, or a stranger, for it would be impossible to trace the offended person in order to obtain his forgiveness, or make restitution to him.

(14) Taking a bribe to give a wrong judgment, or knowingly giving the wrong advice to someone. In such a case it is difficult to measure the extent of the hurt or damage caused to the wronged party, and to make full amends for it.

The following five transgressions are likely to remain without repentance, because they are not considered as transgressions:

(15) Accepting an invitation to share a meal which is not sufficient for both the host and the guest. This has the "tint of robbery" (or, in Hebrew terms, "dust of robbery"), for the invitation is a forced one, the host being ashamed not to invite the guest to a meal, and he is actually depriving himself of food out of this sense of shame. The guest may think that he had done nothing wrong in accepting the invitation, but in fact, such an invitation should not be accepted.

(16) Making use of a pledge left as security for a loan. The creditor may think that he is doing nothing wrong, since the pledge is not harmed thereby. But, in fact, one has no right to use something without the owner's consent.

(17) Committing a sin, not by an actual deed, but merely by the eyes, as, for example, watching an indecent sight. The onlooker may think that he is not *doing* anything wrong, for he is merely watching; but actually the Torah forbids it, as it is written, "And you shall not go astray after your heart and after your eyes."

(18) Gaining honor at the expense of someone else, though with no intention to shame the other, as, for example, when one compares himself to someone else in order to prove to somebody that he is superior.

(19) Casting suspicion on the innocent, though not openly accusing the innocent party; even a mere suggestion or insinuation is a sin, no matter how little one thinks of it.

Finally, Maimonides enumerates five types of transgression, which, if they are committed lightheartedly and frequently, become a bad habit, and the sinner will find it hard to rid himself of them:

(20) Talebearing or "peddling" scandal and malicious hearsay, which is a sin even if the report is true and told without ill-feeling. This includes all kinds of gossip, which one permits himself to hear and to repeat.

(21) Slander (*Lashon-hara*), the sin of the man with the evil tongue who is worse than a murderer, since he destroys a man's reputation, which is more precious than life, and who "kills" with his tongue three victims: himself, the man listening to his slander, and the slandered person.

(22) Anger. The man who becomes easily angered, offended or provoked, is always in danger of doing the most dreadful things, and cause untold harm to himself and others. Besides, a person who becomes easily angered or offended, denies, indirectly, Divine Providence, and that is why anger is likened to "idolatry."

(23) Sinful thinking. Allowing one's thoughts to dwell on sinful things may become a bad habit, and lead to serious crimes.

(24) Associating with bad company may likewise become a habit, bad in itself, and leading to evil doing.

* * *

The great Maimonides warns us especially against all the above twenty-four types of transgressions, since they are of such a nature as to make Teshuvah difficult or even impossible. But this does not mean that there is no hope for the sinner who committed one or more of the above transgressions. It only means that he is faced with many difficulties and hardships on his road to Repentance. But if he is determined, in spite of everything, to purify himself and return to G-d, *there is nothing that stands in the way of Teshuvah,* our Sages assure us.

"THE GOLDEN MEAN"

I wonder if you have ever stopped to consider what sort of nature you have? If you did, would you find that you are too quick-tempered, or too placid? Too mean, or too extravagant? Too gay, or too miserable? Too "anything?"

Here are some of the things that the great Maimonides had to say about the kind of character one should try to possess.

"The 'happy medium' is the right and best way for one to follow," this wise and famous teacher tells us, and he continues:

There are very many opinions that each and every person has, and all differ from each other, and are as far apart from each other as the Poles.

Likewise with character. There is the person who becomes angry in a flash, and another who never, or very rarely, loses his temper. Then there is the proud person, and one who goes to the other extreme and suffers from an "inferiority complex."

There is the person who is so self-indulgent, that he can only think of himself and what he would like for himself. Whilst at the other end, there is the one who thinks too little about himself, to the extent of neglecting his needs.

One sometimes meets someone who is so greedy for money, that he can never seem to get enough to satisfy his lust. And the opposite is the case with one who has so little ambition, that he does not even trouble to acquire sufficient money to cover his most necessary expenses.

A mean person will go without food and drink, so that he can save, and an over-generous one will just let his money slip through his fingers without considering whether he can afford to give it away or not.

People live according to the ideas which have surrounded them from birth, or those they assimilated as they grew up, or maybe adopted after study and careful thought, resulting in the conviction that theirs is the right and true way of life.

Now here is where one should stop to consider if one is, in truth, following the right and true path!

If we find ourselves at any "extreme," we must, in order to gain the "golden mean," swing over to the other "extreme." For, being naturally drawn to where we were accustomed to be, we will most likely, and before long, find ourselves in the "middle," where we must try to remain.

Have you ever watched a "tight-rope" walker? Whenever he looks as if he will fall to one side, he suddenly swings himself over to the other side, and thus regains and keeps his balance!

So we must deal with any of our habits which tend to be extreme, in order to achieve the "happy medium."

Those who go as near as possible to what they consider to be the "ideal" are called "pious," but this is not an easy thing to achieve. That is why we are recommended to follow the "middle path" and we can still earn for ourselves the title "wise," our Sages tell us.

We are commanded to "walk in His ways" which our Rabbis explain as meaning:

"As the Almighty is 'gracious,' we must be gracious.

"As He is 'merciful,' we must be merciful.

"As He is 'holy,' we must also make ourselves holy.

Likewise when our Prophets describe G-d as being "slow to anger," "abounding in loving kindness," "righteous," "upright," and "perfect," they taught us that we must always try to copy Him in these virtues, so that we "walk in His ways."

"Yes," you will say, "it is easy to talk! But it is not so easy to *do* these things!"

Of course it isn't easy, but the easy way is not necessarily the right way. To do right may be difficult at first, but when you have made up your mind that you know what is right and try to carry it out once, twice and thrice, you will find that with each repetition the difficulty becomes less and less formidable, until you have become so used to it, that it isn't hard any more and becomes your good habit.

G-d said about our Patriarch Abraham (Genesis 18, 19):

"For I have known him to the end that he may command his children and his household after him, that they may *keep the way of the Lord,* to do righteousness and justice; to the end that the Lord may bring upon Abraham that which He hath spoken of him."

We, as the children of Abraham, must try and "keep the way of the Lord" and thus earn the fulfillment of His blessing.

OVINU MALKEINU

Rashi* tells us that the "Ovinu Malkeinu" in the form we say it nowadays, is an expansion of the ordinary shorter prayer composed by Rabbi Akiba, of which the Talmud reports: It happened once during a period of drought that Rabbi Eliezer stood before the congregation and said twenty-four prayers for rain, yet without success. No rain came. Then Rabbi Akiba stepped before the congregation and said "Ovinu Malkeinu" and his prayer was immediately answered. When the Sages saw that Rabbi Akiba's "Ovinu Malkeinu" was a very effective prayer, they added further requests to it, and instituted the entire prayer as part of the service for the days of Repentance.

The Levush** tells us that the parts which have been added to the original requests contained in "Ovinu Malkeinu," follow the scheme of the Berachoth of the Shemone Esrei. Therefore it is said right after it.

Since "Ovinu Malkeinu" has been composed similarly to the Shemone Esrei, we have to say it standing and with special attention. Therefore it is also omitted when Rosh

* Rabbi Solomon Yitzchaki, 4800-4865 after Creation.

** Rabbi Mordecai Yoffe, Talmudist and Kabalist, b. Prague 5290; d. Posen 5372.

Hashanah occurs on a Shabbos, just like the Shemone Esrei of the weekdays. Another reason for this omission is that it contains prayers for our personal interests which are to be left out on Shabbos (also during the Minchah service on Erev Shabbos).

The use of the expression "Ovinu Malkeinu," (our Father, our King), has been explained by our Sages as follows: A prince was abducted in his childhood and was taken to a remote country. He can return to his father's land without any shame whatsoever over his long absence whenever he wants to do so, because it is his own heritage to which he returns. Similarly a Jew can always return to the Torah, although he had been estranged from it for many years, because it is his heritage. Therefore we pray: "Bring us back to your Torah, our Father," because G-d will always take us back when we come to Him.

Ovinu Malkeinu: Our Father and our King: As father He has never denied us His love. As king He demands our obedience and controls our fate. During the Ten Days of Repentance these thoughts should bring us back to G-d, and make us throw ourselves down at His feet as His children and His servants confessing: "*Chotonu lefonecho,*" we have sinned before Thee, and begging — *Rachem oleinu,* have mercy upon us.

READING OF THE TORAH ON SHABBOS-SHUVAH

The Sabbath between Rosh-Hashanah and Yom-Kippur is called *Shabbos-Shuvah* ("Return"), after the first word of the Haphtorah. It is sometimes called Shabbos Teshuvah ("Repentance"), being one of the Ten Days of Repentance, the period from Rosh-Hashanah through Yom Kippur. The meaning is the same.

Isn't it significant that Shabbos Teshuvah is *after* and not *before* Rosh-Hashanah? Thus, even after man attains the great spiritual heights of Rosh Hashanah, there is still need for a Shabbos Teshuvah.

For, the closer one comes to G-d, the better he realizes his shortcomings in the service of G-d. Every step forward really means that the last step is way behind, though it was once an "advance." And as man rises ever higher, from one plane to a higher plane, he has reason to repent of his earlier state, when he was further removed from G-d than now.

The reading in the Torah on Shabbos-Shuvah is mostly the portion of *Haazinu,* the last but one in the Five Books of Moses. Sometimes, however, it could be the portion *Vayelech,* i.e., the one preceding *Haazinu.* Both portions contain elements which are quite suitable to the time, such as Moses' rebuke to the children of Israel in taking leave from them, calling for obedience to G-d, repentance, and so on.

The portion *Haazinu* contains the famous Song of Moses. Its beautiful verses contain the secret of Israel's existence and the future of its destiny.

The *Haphtorah* (*Hosea* 14) of this Sabbath is obviously suitable to the character of the day. It is the Sabbath of the Ten Days of Repentance. The Haphtorah, therefore, begins with a call for repentance: "Return, O Israel, unto the Lord thy G-d." It tells us not to rely upon any other people in times of distress, but upon G-d alone. In some congregations the Haphtorah is continued with reading from chapter 2 of Joel, beginning with "Sound the Shofar in Zion," which continues in the same vein as the prophecy of Hosea.

THE COACHMAN

I.

This is the strange but true story of a great scholar who turned coachman in his declining years, because. . . . But let me tell you the whole story.

His name was Joseph, and he lived in a little town in White Russia, called Beshenkovitch. Joseph had spent many years in ardent study of the Talmud, until he became known far beyond his own community. His wife ran a grocery store all by herself, so that her husband could devote all his time to study and have some time left for teaching youngsters. Needless to say, Joseph taught them all free of charge.

Although no longer a young man, Joseph would often walk all the way to Liazno to visit the great Rabbi of that town, Rabbi Schneur Zalman,* to listen to his public discourses and sermons. He became one of the Rabbi's most ardent followers.

One day, when Joseph came in to take leave of the Rabbi, the Rabbi asked him whether he knew any of the six tractates of the Mishnah by heart.

"It is my custom to repeat all the six tractates of the Mishnah by heart in the course of a month, so that during the year I repeat them twelve times, besides my other studies," Joseph replied.

"It is a very great habit," said the Rabbi. "Mishnah contains the letters of 'Neshamah' (soul). To study the Mishnah is very good for the soul. As for *your* soul, it would be better for you to become a coachman, rather than a rabbi."

Joseph was somewhat dazed when he walked out of the Rabbi's presence that time. True, he did not contemplate becoming a Rabbi, but neither did he ever dream of becoming a coachman, of all things! Yet, he knew the Rabbi to be a saintly man, whose words were not to be trifled with.

By the time Joseph returned home, however, he had completely forgotten about the Rabbi's words. He returned to his studies, and his teaching.

Ten years passed by, and Joseph's name became more and more famous.

---

* Rabbi Shneur Zalman of Liadi, author of the "Tanya" and "Shulchan Aruch," founder of Chabad Chassidism. About his life and teachings, see "Rabbi Shneur Zalman of Liadi," published by Kehot Publication Society, Brooklyn, N. Y., 1948.

II.

One day a delegation of prominent Jews from the town of Lepla, not a hundred miles away, came to Joseph, inviting him to become the rabbi and spiritual leader of their community. Joseph was about to accept the invitation, when through his mind flashed the Rabbi's words: "For your soul it is better to become a coachman than a rabbi."

"The Rabbi is truly a seer," Joseph thought, "and the time has come for me to act upon his advice."

Without hesitation, Joseph declined the honor, though he did not tell the delegation the reason.

However, when it came to making a resolution concerning his future, Joseph found that it was not so easy to fulfill the Rabbi's words. He, a great scholar, and in his declining days, to begin to drive a horse and wagon! Why, that's preposterous! People will think he's become touched in his head.

For a few days Joseph suffered great mental agony while he was weighing the matter, now for, now against it. Finally, he mustered up all his courage and went down to the market place where the coaches were stationed. When the coachmen saw him approach, every one greeted him respectfully, and offered to take him wherever he wanted to go.

"No, my friends, I have no intention of going any place. I merely came, er . . . to get acquainted with your profession," Joseph said bashfully.

The coachmen exchanged curious glances, and looked upon Joseph, wondering whether they understood him clearly.

"It's not like you, Rabbi Joseph, to jest," one of them finally said.

"But I am not jesting," Joseph said, his eyes downcast.

Still the coachmen did not believe him. Some of them thought the old man had lost his wits. Finally, one of them approached him and said earnestly, "Follow me to the stable, Rabbi Joseph, and I will teach you the art."

Joseph followed. The coachman showed Joseph how to harness the horse, grease the wheels. and so forth. Poor Joseph was not accustomed to it. He got himself thoroughly dirty, and nearly lost an eye when the horse lashed him with his tail.

Dirty and dejected, Joseph came home. He washed himself and changed his clothes, and went to *shul* for the Minchah service, after which he was to give his daily discourse on the Talmud. Every one looked at him sympathetically.

When Joseph came home that night, he noticed his wife's eyes were red from weeping. She must have heard all about it. Joseph went to his room and wept too. Finally he decided to follow the advice of the Sages, and share his problem with his wife. He told her why he tried to learn the trade of coachman.

Far from feeling unhappy, his wife replied almost cheerfully:

"If the saintly Rabbi told you to do so, what problem can there be? Tomorrow I shall sell my jewels so that you can buy yourself a horse and cart."

For a moment Joseph looked at his wife in astonishment. Her matter-of-fact attitude, simple faith and complete confidence in the Rabbi's words left him speechless. Joseph felt ashamed of himself, and a feeling of remorse filled his heart. However, all doubts had been dispelled, and his mind was made up. The following day he bought a horse and coach. . . .

III.

One day, Joseph was on his way to the town of Senna, with a load of merchandise. When night fell, Joseph decided to stay overnight at the nearest inn on the road. The innkeeper was a Jew, and Joseph made himself quite at home there. A little while later the Count of Batzeikov with his suite arrived at the same inn, and decided to spend the night there. However, when word reached the nearest village that the Count was at the inn, the priest came to invite him to his house. The Count could not turn down his request, and accompanied him. His Jewish manager, however, stayed at the inn, intending to proceed to Senna the following morning.

Joseph was busy studying the Talmud, but when he finished and closed the Gemara, the innkeeper introduced him to the manager, whose name was Solomon Gametzky, saying he wanted to go to Senna.

"Very good, Sir," Joseph said. "I'll be glad to take you to Senna tomorrow morning."

"What time?" Gametzky asked.

"After prayers," was the reply.

"You can pray as much as you want," Gametzky said unkindly. "I must leave early, and must know the exact time when to get up, so that I can get washed and eat without hurry."

" . . . and pray," Joseph said for him.

"Keep your prayers to yourself," Gametzky retorted.

"How can a Jew talk like this?" Joseph reproached his would-be-customer. "How can a Jew do without prayers? And what about the sacred Mitzvah of Tefillin? Some scholarly opinion holds that Tefillin are really two Mitzvoth in one!"

Solomon Gametzky did not say anything more. Having ordered the innkeeper to get him another coach for five o'clock in the morning, he retired without saying "good night."

Joseph also retired, after he had said his evening prayers and had supper. But at midnight he got up again to pray *chatzoth* (midnight prayers) as he was used to do.

The sound of Joseph's prayers and supplications broke the stillness of the night.

The Count's manager fell asleep with a strange heaviness in his head. He woke up with a start and sat up in bed to listen. It was a familiar voice, and for a moment he thought it was his deceased father's. Gametzky recalled what a fine and venerable Jew his father was, and that he also used to get up at midnight to pray in exactly the same manner as this coachman. . . .

On and on Joseph prayed, and his prayers and supplications were so moving, that the manager sat entranced. He now recalled his youth very clearly, as though it were projected on a screen before his eyes. He saw his beloved father, a pious man, who, together with the Rabbi of the community, shared in the greatest honor accorded to men of learning and piety. He recalled the delightful way of life, so quiet and harmonious, which he had been leading in those days, until he met that horrible boy who led him astray, and persuaded him to run away from home . . . To be sure, he made himself a "fine career"; he made friends with the Count, and had become his personal secretary and manager; together they drank a great deal and made merry, but he knew his spiritual life had been an empty one all the time. His soul was yearning for that enchanting Jewish environment in which he had grown up. . . .

A knock at the door roused him from his trance. Gametzky found his cheeks wet, for unconsciously tears had been rolling down his face. He wiped them off quickly, and called out, "Yes? What is it?"

"Your new coachman is here, Sir," the innkeeper replied.

"I am not going with him. Pay him off well. I'll wait for Joseph," Gametzky said.

Solomon Gametzky got dressed, and went out to borrow a Tallith, a pair of Tefillin and a Siddur from the innkeeper. He returned back to his room to pray. Never had he prayed with so much feeling as this time. He made a firm resolution that from now on he would become an observant Jew with all his heart and soul.

That providential meeting with Joseph was a turning point in Gametzky's life.

Solomon Gametzky did not return to his position. He asked the Count to accept his resignation, and this was granted him. He became Joseph's best friend; together they studied, and together they went to Lubavitz, where the Old Rabbi's son was the spiritual leader, in the place of his father.

When Joseph entered the study of the Rabbi, the Rabbi said to him: "My father told me that you have fulfilled your mission, for which he had made you a coachman. There is no further need of your remaining a coachman. I appoint you spiritual leader in Beshenkovitch."

Rabbi Joseph sold his horse and coach, and for many years was the beloved teacher and spiritual leader of his congregation in Beshenkovitch, reaching a very ripe old age. He never regretted those hard years, when he drove his horse and cart around, for he was very happy to have helped a lost fellow-Jew return to his faith and his people.

IN APPRECIATION

The story is told of a great and saintly Rabbi who was once asked by a Jew: "Rabbi, why do you look so ill? Are you sick?"

"No," replied the saintly Rabbi, "it is because I have been put to shame by a certain person."

"How could any one dare to do such a thing to you! Please tell me who it was!"

The Rabbi replied that he could not tell him the name of the person. The Jew was persistent, however, and asked the Rabbi:

"Tell me then, Rabbi, what did you do to the man after he had insulted you?"

"I embraced him and kissed him," came the astonishing reply.

The Jew could not restrain himself any longer and begged the Rabbi to give him the name of this person whom he treated so contrarily, kissing and embracing him as a reward for putting him to shame!

"It was Rabbi Elijah HaCohen,* the author of 'Shevet-Mussar' (Rod of Admonition) who put me to shame. I had become deeply interested in his book and then it dawned upon me that I had not even begun to serve the Almighty sufficiently, that I was not worthy of being a descendant of Abraham, Isaac and Jacob, and I felt very much ashamed of myself.

"I realized the truth of all he had written, and then in my appreciation and gratitude to him for showing me the truth, I took his book and kissed it."

---

* Famous Rabbi and Preacher at Smyrna (Turkish *Izmir*); d. 5489 (1729).

THE DAY OF ATONEMENT

THE HOLIEST DAY

Erev-Yom-Kippur

EREV-YOM-KIPPUR is ushered in by that age-old custom of "kapparoth" (atonement). A man or boy takes a rooster, a woman or girl—a hen, in his or her hand, reciting the prayer "Bnai-odom" (children of man), and swinging the fowl over the head a certain prayer is recited: "Be this my atonement," etc. The idea of this custom is to evoke sincere repentance through the thought that a similar fate as that awaiting the fowl might be due to us for our sins, but for G-d's mercy to forgive us upon our true repentance. The fowl is then dropped under the table, and is soon sent to the "*shoichet*," and the meat, or the value of it, is given to the poor.

This custom may be observed also with money.

At the morning service there is another charming little custom: The synagogue warden, or the "Gabbai," distributes pieces of cake to the worshippers. The symbolic meaning of it is the thought: "If it were indeed destined that I receive food from charity, may it have been fulfilled just now, and may I never have to beg charity again." This is a very humble thought that should make us think of the unfortunate poor, and should make us feel grateful to G-d for having made us a giver rather than a taker as far as charity is concerned.

Minchah is usually *davvened* early in the afternoon to leave ample time for the Erev Yom-Kippur meal. A whole variety of platters representing various charities, notably Yeshivoth, orphanages, etc., greet us at the entrance to the synagogue — a timely reminder of the great Mitzvah of "Tzdakah" — charity.

The Minchah service is said with great humility and repentance, and in the *Shemone-Esrei—Al chet* is said (the long confession of sins committed, knowingly or unknowingly, during the year).

On Erev Yom-Kippur it is a Mitzvah to eat more than usual, and this makes the contrast between that day and the following day of Atonement all the greater. Grace is said very devoutly, and such words as "we beseech thee, do not cause us to be in need of the gifts of man . . ." remind us how dependent we are on G-d's grace.

Then follows the traditional blessing of the children, the father putting his hands on the head of each child, whispering a prayer in his or her behalf, with tears in his eyes. The air seems to be charged with solemnity and awe which seem to grow as the day draws to an end.

Kol-Nidrei

Arriving in *shul* we remove our shoes and put on the Tallith, when it is still daytime. Service begins with the taking out of Torah Scrolls by venerable members of the community, who then take up a place on each side of the *Chazan* (cantor). The *Chazan* then slowly recites the *Kol Nidrei* three times in that special Kol-Nidrei tune so well known to us, and all the worshippers inaudibly repeat each word after him.

The evening service follows the Kol Nidrei prayer, with special additional prayers which are said only on the night of Yom-Kippur.

Yom-Kippur

The Morning Service (*Shacharith*) is begun fairly early. The prayers are recited slowly and carefully from the *machzor*. For the reading of the Torah two scrolls are taken from the Ark. In the first — the beginning of

Achrei Moth ("after the death" — of Aaron's two sons) is read. It is said, that who sincerely sheds tears on the great loss of Aaron's two sons will not suffer any such bereavement in his lifetime! This portion tells of the Yom-Kippur sacrifice and service by the High Priest in the Holy Temple.

"Yizkor" (May He remember) is recited after the reading of the Torah, when the dear departed are remembered in a special prayer. Those fortunate worshippers whose parents are still living, leave the *shul* at this prayer, but the others shed many a tear remembering their beloved father and mother. Many of them cannot help feeling remorseful at the thought how they had drifted away from the beautiful traditional way of life that their dear parents and grandparents had led; they know their parents would like them to be more loyal and more devoted to the Torah and tradition, and they really resolve to please them in the future much more than in the past.

The "*Musaph*" prayer is then recited, beginning with the moving prayer of *Hineni* ("Here I am a poor man, destitute of good deeds," etc.) recited by the *Chazan.*

The Musaph prayer of Yom-Kippur includes a recital of the way the High Priest used to officiate at the Holy Temple on Yom-Kippur and the special confession and atonement he offered in behalf of the people of Israel. It was an unforgettable sight to see him in his white robes coming out of the Holy of Holies where he was permitted to enter only on this day of the whole year.

There is usually a small interval between *Musaph* and *Minchah.* The outstanding feature of the *Minchah* service is the reading of the Torah, and especially of *Maftir,* when the celebrated book of Jonah is recited, which tells of the saving of the great city of Nineveh through timely repentance.

Ne'ila

After *Minchah* follows the very solemn *Ne'ila* (Closing) service, which is the climax of all the Yom-Kippur prayers. The Ark is kept open throughout this prayer. The Ne'ila service is concluded with the exclamation of *Shema* and *Boruch Shem,* our proclamation of undaunted loyalty and determination to die for our faith if necessary, as our sacred martyrs did in the past. This is followed by that famous declaration of G-d's unity: "G-d — He is the Only G-d," first said at Mt. Carmel by our prophet Elijah. This last verse is repeated seven times in the most ardent way. The Shofar is then sounded one long *Tekiah,* and the Holy Day (like the Seder) is concluded with the prayer, "Next Year may we be in Jerusalem!"

Maariv and *Habdalah* usher in the short interval of four days until the arrival of Succoth. "Good Yomtov" is the greeting after *Maariv,* and everybody feels happy and confident that our good G-d has surely accepted our prayers and has "inscribed and sealed us" all unto a happy year.

If the moon can be seen, it is customary to say the prayer of "Kiddush Levana," without regret at having to prolong the fast for another few minutes. . . .

After breaking the fast, it is customary to make the first preparations for the building of a Succah, as a gesture of our eagerness to do a *Mitzvah.*

THE DAY OF ATONEMENT IN THE BETH HAMIKDOSH OF OLD

(*From the Mishnah, Yoma*)

Seven days before the Day of Atonement the High Priest was separated from his home and taken unto the Counsellors' Chamber (*Lishkath Palhedrin*) and another priest was made ready to take his place in case anything should befall him which would render him unfit for the Service.

He was placed in care of the elders of the Court (*Beth-Din*), and they read before him the order of the day (to make him well versed in the service). And they said unto him: "My Lord High Priest, do thou thyself recite with thine own mouth, lest thou hast forgotten, or lest thou hast never learnt."

On the eve of the Day of Atonement in the morning they make him stand at the Eastern Gate and pass before him oxen, rams, and sheep, that he may gain knowledge and become versed in the Service.

Throughout the seven days they did not withhold food and drink from him; but on the eve of the Day of Atonement, towards nightfall, they did not permit him to eat much, since food induces sleep.

The elders of the Court delivered him to the elders of the priesthood, and they brought him up to the House of Abtinas (in the upper story of the Beth Hamikdosh, on the south side of the "Court of the Priests"). They made him pledge an oath that he should perform the Service according to Tradition, and before leaving him said unto him: "My Lord High Priest, we are delegates of the Court, and thou art our delegate and the delegate of the Court. We adjure thee by Him that made His Name dwell in this House that thou change naught of what we have said unto thee." He turned aside and wept, and they turned aside and wept (for a suspicion had been cast upon him).

If he was a Sage he used to expound the Scriptures, and if not, the Sages used to expound before him. If he was versed in reading the Scriptures, he read, and if not, they read before him (to divert the mind and drive away sleep). And from what did they read before him? Out of Job and Ezra and Chronicles. Zechariah ben Kebutal said, "Many times I read before him out of Daniel."

If he appeared sleepy, young members of the priesthood would snap their middle finger before him and say to him, "My Lord High Priest, get up and drive away sleep this once by walking on the cold pavement." And they used to divert him until the time of the sacrifice drew near.

Lots were cast to divide the sacred services among the priests.

The officer in charge said to him, "Go and see if the time is come for the sacrifice." If it was come, he that saw it, called out "Barkai!" ("It is daylight").

The High Priest was taken to the place of immersion. On this day the High Priest five times immerses himself and ten times he sanctifies his hands and his feet.

They spread a linen sheet between him and the people. He stripped off his clothes, went down and immersed himself, came up and dried himself. They brought him raiments of gold and he put them on and sanctified his hands and his feet. They brought to him the Daily Whole-offering (*Tamid*). He made the incision and another completed the offering on his behalf. He went inside to burn the morning incense and to trim the lamps.

They brought him to the Parwah Chamber (within the Court of the Beth Hamikdosh). They spread a linen sheet between him and the people. He sanctified his hands and his feet and stripped off his clothes. He went down and immersed himself, came up and dried himself. They brought him white garments; he put them on and sanctified his hands and his feet.

In the morning he was clothed in Pelusium linen worth twelve *minas*, and in the afternoon in Indian linen worth eight hundred *zuz*. This was paid for from public funds, and if he wished to spend more, he could do so at his own expense.

He came to his bullock, which was standing between the Hall and the Altar, its head to the south and its face turned to the west. And the Priest stood in the east with his face to the west; and he placed his hands upon it and made confession. And thus used he to say, "O G-d, I have committed iniquity, transgressed and sinned before Thee, I and my house. O G-d, forgive the iniquities and transgressions and sins which I have committed and transgressed and sinned before Thee, I and my house, as it is written in the Torah of Thy servant Moses, 'For on this day shall atonement be made for you to cleanse you; from all your sins before G-d shall ye be clean.' "

* * *

And the priests and the people who stood in the Court, when they heard the glorious, awe-inspiring and ineffable Name come forth from the mouth of the High Priest with sanctity and purity, they kneeled and prostrated themselves, and fell on their faces, saying, "Blessed be the Name of His glorious Majesty for ever and ever."

* * *

After the Service of the day was over, they brought

him his own garments, which he put on, and they accompanied him to his house. And he made a festival for all his friends, to celebrate his leaving the Sanctuary without any mishap.

* * *

How glorious was the High Priest, when he came forth safe from the Sanctuary. . . .

Even as the expanded canopy of the heaven, was the countenance of the Priest.

As the lightning that proceedeth from the splendor of the angels, was the countenance of the Priest. . . .

As the appearance of rainbow in the midst of the cloud. . . .

As the rose in the midst of a delightful garden. . . .

As the tenderness depicted on the face of a bridegroom. . . .

As the golden bells in the skirts of the mantle. . . .

As the appearance of the rising sun on the earth. . . .

Happy the eye which saw all these things.

(*From the Machzor*)

A BLESSING IN TIME

Father loved to play with his little son, for he loved him dearly. Once he brought him a beautiful apple, but did not give it to him at once. As the little boy stretched out his hand to snatch the apple, father drew it away quickly. The boy tried again, and again the apple was way above his head. This was repeated several times in a playful way, but the boy really wanted to have the apple, yet could not get it immediately.

Now the boy was a clever little fellow. He thought of a way to make his father give him the apple at once. Can you guess what he did?

When father pulled the apple away from him again, the boy suddenly said the blessing over fruit, which he knew very well, as all good little boys should. The father had no choice but to give him the apple to eat immediately, otherwise the blessing would have been said in vain!

* * *

Something like this we also do on Yom-Kippur, the Day of Atonement, when we fast and pray to G-d to forgive us our sins. In our prayers on that day we say a blessing, praising G-d as the "King who pardons and forgives our sins."

Now G-d would not want us to say a false blessing. So He forgives us, if we really want Him to. But in order to receive G-d's pardon, we must feel sorry for anything wrong we may have done, and promise with all our hearts never to do anything wrong again.

READINGS FROM THE TORAH ON YOM-KIPPUR

In the Morning:
Portion: Leviticus 16
Haphtorah: Isaiah 57

Two scrolls are taken out on Yom Kippur for the reading during the Morning Service. In the first, six men are called up to read (and on a Sabbath — seven), after which Maftir is read in the second.

The reading in the Torah is about the solemn service in the Beth Hamikdosh, on the Day of Atonement, conducted by the High Priest himself. This was the only day in the year when the High Priest was permitted to enter the Holy of Holies to offer incense and recite a prayer there in behalf of the entire people.

The Haphtorah speaks of the true meaning of repentance. The prophet calls for a clearing of the path of repentance. Though G-d is exalted and dwells on High, the prophet says, He is also with the contrite and humble of spirit. G-d proclaims peace to him that is far and to him that is near, and assures all of healing of the spirit. But fasting alone is not enough. "Verily this fast I choose: to dissolve the bands of wickedness . . . to distribute the bread to the hungry . . . when thou seest the naked clothe him, and hide not thyself from thine own flesh." But still this is not all. No repentance can be complete without a better appreciation and observance of the holy Sabbath: "If thy feet rest on the Sabbath from following thy occupation on My holy day; and thou shalt call the Sabbath a delight . . . and thou shalt honor it by refraining from thy usual ways, from pursuing thy pleasure and from speaking vain words—then shalt thou find delight in the Lord. . . ."

In the Afternoon:

Portion: LEVITICUS 18

Haphtorah: BOOK OF JONAH

The reading in the Torah for the Minchah service of the Day of Atonement speaks of the purity of Jewish life. The Torah warns us not to follow in the immoral ways of the Egyptians and native Canaanites, "that the land spue you not out also, when ye defile it, as it spued out the nations that were before you."

The Haphtorah consists of the whole Book of Jonah, the story of which is surely familiar to you. It contains a timely message on the importance of repentance and prayer. If sinfulness causes the land to vomit its inhabitants, repentance caused the fish to vomit Jonah back on dry land and return him to life. Never should anyone despair. Prayer and repentance lead from darkness to light, from the shadow of death to a new life.

LET'S VISIT NINEVEH

Nineveh is not a Jewish city, but the name is familiar to most Jewish children. In the book of the prophet Jonah, which we read as the Haphtorah of the Minchah service of Yom-Kippur, Nineveh is the center of interest. The story of the Book of Jonah is well known, and we need not dwell on it. The interest of this story is centered on "Teshuvah" (repentance), and the lesson it teaches us is a very timely one on the occasion of the Day of Atonement.

About a hundred years ago, if a boy asked the teacher during a lesson on the Book of Jonah, or Nachum, or Zephaniah (for all three Prophets mention this city), "Where is Nineveh? Can one visit the city nowadays?" the teacher would have had to answer, "We know very little about the location of the city." Today, however, we are more fortunate. For in the past hundred years explorers of antiquity have excavated much of the once beautiful and powerful capital of the great Assyrian empire.

To get to Nineveh nowadays is not difficult. All we have to do is to start from Haifa, in the Land of Israel, and simply follow the famous oil pipe-line all the way to Mosul, in Iraq. There, across the Tigris River, on the left bank, opposite Mosul, lie the ruins of the once proud city of Nineveh.

Nineveh was one of the first cities ever built. Chumash tells us that it was built by king Nimrod (also called Ashur), the father of the Assyrian people. That was in the time of Abraham. It must have grown steadily, and it became the capital of the Assyrian Empire, about three thousand years ago. Under the powerful Assyrian kings the city was enlarged and beautified. Sargon built a strong wall around Nineveh, including and uniting it with three other cities. It was this enlarged city that the Prophet Jonah speaks of as a city of "three days' journey."

Under Sennacherib the city was further enlarged and beautified. Sennacherib built great palaces in it. One of the castles he built, and which was only excavated partially, contained as many as seventy-one large, and beautifully decorated rooms. Sennacherib also erected arsenals for military purposes, strengthened the forts which guarded every part of the long walls. He provided the city with a most astonishing aqueduct which provided water for the city through eighteen separate channels from the hills. In the center of the city, Sennacherib, who must have had an unusual understanding of city planning, planted the "Paradise," a huge park in which grew trees, plants and flowers of the entire world. Around these "Botanical Gardens" no one was permitted to build houses or workshops.

Ashurbanipal vied with Sennacherib in making Nineveh the jewel-city of the east. Most important of his constructions is the greatest library of old, which was recently excavated, and in which were found tens of thousands of clay tablets containing the entire Babylonian and most of the world's literature. The excellent order and care of the library is astonishing.

At the time of Jonah, Nineveh was a center of immorality and depravity. One can easily understand the Prophet Jonah when he refused to step into this humming, elegant world capital to tell the people that they should do "Teshuvah," repentance, otherwise they would be destroyed. And one can even better understand the surprise of the prophet that his words had made an impression upon the proud inhabitants of the Assyrian metropolis. For the inhabitants of Nineveh, from king to slave, changed their evil ways and returned to the ways of G-d, regretting deeply, with sackcloth and ashes upon their heads, their previous mode of living. This was truly an event which the world was not destined to see again throughout history.

But the short period of repentance in the days of Jonah passed, and Nineveh returned to its wicked ways.

The end of Nineveh was inevitable, as Nachum and Zephaniah predicted: "The doom of Nineveh, the city of blood. It is full of lies and robbery; never ceaseth preying . . . O, king of Assyria, there is no healing for thy breach; fatal is thy wound: all that hear the report of thee will clap their hands over thee; for over whom did not thy wickedness pass continually!"

About the year 612 before the common era, the city was besieged by the Babylonians and Medes, and destroyed completely, never again to be inhabited.

The mighty Assyrian empire, which had destroyed the Northern Kingdom of Israel, met with its retribution. Nineveh was wiped off the face of the earth, and its ruins can serve as an eloquent commentary on what happens to all the proud and mighty.

Rabbi Tachlifah taught: All of a man's earnings during the year to come are determined during the period of Rosh-Hashanah through Yom-Kippur, save the expenses for the Sabbath and the festivals and the tuition fees spent on teaching the children Torah. These expenses are not determined in advance, so that if one spends more on these things, more is given to him, and if less—less is given to him.

(*Talmud Babli,* Betzah 16a)

EREV-YOM-KIPPUR BIDDING

In ancient Rome there lived a Jewish tailor. He worked very hard, and lived simply and modestly. Most of his savings from the whole week's earnings he would spend on Shabbos and Yomtov, which he held in great esteem and honor. One day, it was *Erev-Yom-Kippur,* the tailor went to the market to buy fish for the day's special meal, knowing that it was a great Mitzvah to honor the day with a feast, and fish was especially fitting for the occasion.

He searched the whole market, but there was no fish to be had. Finally, he found a fisherman who had one large fish to sell. The tailor was very happy, and took out his purse to pay whatever the fisherman asked. At that very moment a man came up clad in a livery, and looking very important.

"Hey, fisherman!" the stranger called. "How much do you want for the fish?"

"But this Jew came first, my lord. I'll sell it to him if he will pay my price," the fisherman replied.

"I will pay any price you say," the tailor hastened to put in.

"But do you know who I am? I am the Lord Mayor's steward! Besides, I'll pay you more than the Jew," the liveried steward said emphatically.

The fisherman was at a loss what to do. In the meantime a crowd gathered and watched the dispute with great curiosity. Someone from the crowd shouted: "Sell it to the highest bidder!"

"I'll give you a whole *dinnar!*" the steward exclaimed, hoping to silence the Jewish tailor at once, and to impress the crowd at the same time.

"What a fortune to bid for a simple fish!" some people in the crowd exclaimed with amazement. But before they got over their surprise, the tailor made his bid:

"Two dinnars," he said quietly.

"Two dinnars!" the crowd roared. "Did you hear that? Two dinnars!"

"Three!" bid the steward.

"Four!" bid the tailor.

"Five!" bid the steward, plainly showing his irritation and annoyance.

"Six!" bid the tailor.

Thus the bidding went on, until the tailor bid no less than twelve dinnars for the fish! At this point the steward gave up, fearing that his master would think him insane if he brought him a fish at such an unheard-of price.

The tailor paid the money, got the fish, and went home to prepare it for the Erev Yom Kippur feast.

When the steward returned to his master without fish, and told him what happened in the market, the Mayor sent for the Jewish tailor.

"How come you paid such a price for a fish?" the Mayor asked.

"To-day is a sacred day for us Jews, my lord," the tailor replied. "It is the day before Yom-Kippur, when our G-d forgives our sins if we repent of them sincerely. On Yom-Kippur we fast, but the day before must be honored with special feasts. Twelve dinnars was all that I had saved up, but when it comes to a Mitzvah, it cannot be measured in terms of money. . . ."

The sincerity of the Jewish tailor, and his devotion to his religion, made a profound impression upon the Mayor, and he let him go home unharmed.

Little did the poor tailor know what reward awaited him there. When his wife opened the fish, she found a large pearl inside!

"G-d has truly rewarded us," the tailor said.

Thereafter, they lived in comfort for the rest of their lives, and every year, when Erev-Yom-Kippur came around, they would observe it even with greater honor than ever before.

THE MYSTERIOUS VISITOR

Many years ago, in the old city of Hebron, on the road to the Cave of Machpelah, there was a small Jewish settlement. So few adult males lived there, that they did not even have a regular "Minyan" for Shabbos.

Only occasionally, if they were fortunate enough to "catch" a Jew or Jews visiting the famous, historic Cave of Machpelah, did they manage to "davven" with a Minyan. At such times the Jews of the settlement were simply overjoyed, for they were very anxious to serve G-d in the best way they could.

One year, they were particularly troubled because Yom-Kippur was approaching with no prospect of being able to get a Minyan together.

The day of Erev-Yom-Kippur came, and they were still one Jew short of the required ten to make up a congregation.

The Jews of the settlement began to feel desperate, and busy as they were, they scattered towards all the main roads, hoping against hope that even at this late hour a miracle would happen and they would find a tenth Jew to complete the Minyan.

The sun was rapidly sinking, as their hearts too were sinking, and they returned home and prepared to go to their small Shul to *davven,* Minyan or no Minyan.

The man who was acting as Chazan was just about to

begin the prayer when, to the astonishment of all present, in walked an old Jew, dressed in old, plain clothes, his back bent, with a sack slung over his shoulder.

They all felt like embracing him, but the hour was too serious for such things. Their thoughts all concentrated on the sacred chanting of the age-old, haunting melodies and soulful prayers.

The Shamash would have liked to have talked to this mysterious visitor after the Service was over, but the stranger seemed so deep in his thoughts and prayers, that the Shamash decided to leave him undisturbed.

The visitor spent the night in Shul as did most of the other worshippers. As you have already learned, the Jews of the settlement were very pious and G-d fearing, and they humbly thanked the Almighty for having graciously answered their prayer by sending them a tenth Jew, so that they could *davven* with a Minyan on this holiest of days—Yom-Kippur.

As soon as Yom-Kippur was over, there was almost a rush to get to the strange old man who had appeared like an angel from heaven. Everyone wanted to have the honor of taking him home with them to break the fast. They almost began to quarrel, till the Shamash very wisely suggested that the fairest solution would be to "cast lots." Everyone agreed. To the great joy of the Shamash, who was a great Torah scholar, he was the lucky one to have the honor of being host to their visitor.

The Shamash was anxious to please his guest, and did not bother him with questions. All that the Shamash was able to get out of the old man was that his name was Abraham. They walked out of Shul together, and the Shamash was satisfied to carry on a more or less one-sided conversation.

All of a sudden the Shamash felt an ominous stillness and, peering in the darkness of the night, he realized he

was alone! His guest had disappeared!

Horror of horrors! What had happened to Abraham?

"Abraham! Abraham!" the Shamash called out, frantically running this way and that. But there was no response, and no sign of Abraham.

Sadly, and with a heavy heart of misgiving, the Shamash quickly retraced his steps and told the Jews who were on their way home from Shul, of the terrible thing that had happened.

The poor Shamash was desolate. The good Jews of the settlement were as concerned as the Shamash to find their lost visitor, so they all set out with torches, afraid he might have stumbled into a well, or came to grief, G-d forbid.

After hours of searching without results, they all turned sadly home. The Shamash, though, could find no rest, and only as dawn was breaking, did he finally fall into a troubled sleep, out of sheer exhaustion.

He had hardly closed his eyes, it seemed to him, when Abraham appeared to him. But now he was most beautifully dressed and he looked radiant.

"Do not worry, my friend," he said gently to the Shamash. "As you see, I am perfectly alright. I am the Patriarch Abraham.

"Your prayers reached me here in the Cave of Machpelah and I came to you so that you should have the spiritual satisfaction of *davvening* on Yom-Kippur with a Minyan.

"As soon as my mission was over, I returned here to my resting place. Go back to your friends and tell them not to worry. No harm has befallen me. I am at peace. Peace be with you."

As soon as the words were spoken, the vision disappeared and the Shamash awoke.

He could hardly get to Shul fast enough to inform

his fellow-Jews of the wonderful dream he had just had.

At first they could hardly believe him, but they knew him to be a pious man so they could have no doubt that it was indeed the Patriarch Abraham who had come to be the tenth man to their Minyan.

Their hearts were filled with a great and abounding joy. Humbly they gave thanks to the Almighty — the G-d of their father Abraham.

THE OPEN MACHZOR

(*A Story*)

It was Yom Kippur Eve. A breathless hush took hold of the congregation as all eyes turned upon the figure of their revered "Baal Shem Tov." He stood there, dressed in his white "Kittel" and wrapped in his Tallith which covered also his bent head. As everyone waited whilst the Baal Shem Tov prepared himself for the sacred prayer of "Kol Nidrei," those nearer to him saw a shadow pass over his face, but no one dared ask him what was wrong.

His obvious distress was reflected in the faces of all present, as they recited the very moving Kol Nidrei prayer. During the brief pause between Kol Nidrei and Maariv, the Baal Shem Tov again became sunk in thought. Suddenly, a gentle smile lit up his face and, as he asked that Maariv be said, everyone present felt a relief which they did not understand. They did not know the reason for their beloved Rabbi's earlier distress, nor did they know the reason why he smiled. All they knew was that whatever affected their saintly leader, also deeply affected each and every one of them.

At the conclusion of Yom Kippur, the Baal Shem Tov told his followers the following story:

My friends, he said, I am going to tell you what affected me so deeply last night during the 'davvening.' The story is connected with a Jewish innkeeper in a nearby village. The innkeeper was a very fine, honest and orthodox Jew whom the landlord, a Polish nobleman, greatly admired and treated as a personal friend. Suddenly, without any warning illness, the innkeeper died, leaving behind him a young widow with a baby boy. The poor young woman became deeply affected by her loss, and before long, she, too died.

The Polish nobleman was very upset about the passing of his tenant and friend, and when the widow also died, he felt it his duty to take the baby into his care now that it was a helpless orphan. He was a very kind man and gave the baby the best care and brought him up as his own son.

Years passed and the child did not know that he was not, in truth, the real son of the Christian nobleman. One day, however, the nobleman had invited some friends of his to visit him at his estate, and whilst their children were playing together in the garden, one of them in the course of a quarrel called the nobleman's "son" a Jew. The boy quickly ran up to the nobleman crying, and asked him if it were really true that he is a Jew?

"My dear boy," he replied gently. "You know how much I love you and that I have treated you as if you were my very own son. When I die you will be my heir; I'll leave everything to you — my estate, my orchards and my forests. What more could I do for you?"

"So I'm not your real son! So I am a Jew and you never told me," the boy burst out sobbing. "Who were my parents? I have to know, please!"

The nobleman put his arms around the boy's shoulders trying to comfort him. "My boy, you can be proud of your parents. They were very fine people indeed; good, G-d fearing Jews. Your father was my friend. It was for his sake that I felt it my duty to take you into my home and bring you up as I would my own son. But you know I have no other children and I love you very dearly."

Bit by bit the boy got the whole story of his own poor Jewish parents. The nobleman told him that his parents had nothing at all to leave him excepting a small package which he had hidden away in a safe place, waiting for the right moment to give it to him. The moment had now come and so he went and brought the package and gave it to the boy. With trembling hands and a quickly beating heart the boy opened the package and beheld an old black velvet bag with strange gold lettering on it. He opened the bag and took out a white wool shawl, something else which looked like two small black boxes wound around with black leather straps, and a book. Of course the boy did not know what the Tallith and Tefillin were, nor could he understand what was in the thick "book" which was a Machzor. But because these precious things had once belonged to his parents, his real parents, whom he had never known, he meant to treasure them as long as he lived!

By a lucky chance the nobleman had to leave on a business trip, which gave the boy a chance to think in peace and quiet. He took long walks in the woods and spent hours thinking. He realized that he loved the nobleman and was grateful to him, and yet — a strange feeling took hold of him which urged him to seek out his Jewish brethren. He knew there were some who lived on his "father's" estates. He would go and see them; talk to them. Perhaps some of them even remembered his parents!

That night he dreamt that his parents came to him, first his father, then his mother. They told him he was now no more a child. He must know he is a Jew and go back to his Jewish people where he belongs.

The next day, very early, he quickly crept out of the house so that none of the servants should stop him or question him. He walked until he reached the next village where he saw some Jews packing some bundles onto carts.

"Good day to you," he called to them. "Are you going to a fair?"

"No, not this time," they replied. "It will soon be our holy festival Yom-Kippur, so we are taking our families to the next big town, so that at least at this sacred time we can all pray in the synagogue with other Jews."

The boy returned home lost in thought. Why had he not taken his parents' gift with him to show to these Jews? They would have told him what they were for. The thought gave him no rest. Also, what was Yom-Kippur?

A few days went by and the nobleman had not yet returned. The boy suddenly decided he was old enough to make up his own mind about this thing which affected his very future. He was a Jew and he meant to go back to his people! So he packed a few clothes together, took some food along, left a note telling his "father" where he had gone, and set off for the town to which the village Jews had said they were going.

After several weary days of travelling, getting a "hitch" when he could, but mostly walking, he finally reached his destination. He found out where the *Shul* was and reached it just as the haunting notes of the Kol Nidrei service were being sung. Quietly the boy slipped inside and took a place near the door. The scene which met his gaze filled him with awe. He looked around him and beheld Jews of all ages praying with all their hearts, some with tears in their eyes. He felt a lump come into his own throat as he quietly took out his own white shawl and wrapped it around his shoulders. He took out his book and tried to hold it as he saw the others holding theirs. But when he opened it and could neither read nor understand the words, sobs suddenly shook his young body.

With the tears streaming down his cheeks, the lad cried out: "O, G-d! You know I cannot read, nor do I know what to say and how to pray. I am just a lost Jewish boy! Here is the whole Prayer-Book! Please dear G-d, take out the right words to form the prayers for me!"

The despair of this poor Jewish lad reached the Heavenly Court on High, and the gates were flung open for his prayer. And together with his simple prayer, our prayers, too, were accepted.

* * *

When the Baal Shem Tov finished this moving story, tears stood in the eyes of all his listeners. And often, when praying, they thought about this strange story of the young Jewish lad who had been lost for a time. And they thought of themselves that they, too, were often like lost souls who did not really know how to pray as well as they should. They all earnestly hoped, like the boy, that the kind and merciful G-d on High would accept their prayers, and grant each and all a truly happy new year, for the important thing about prayer is, after all, the sincerity and devotion to G-d, which come from the heart.

THE MARRANOS CELEBRATE YOM KIPPUR IN AMSTERDAM

Two ships were drifting helplessly in the North Sea. High winds and stormy seas damaged the rudders, and the ships were at the mercy of the storm. Fortunately, the ships were driven towards the shores of the Netherlands, and finally found shelter in a Dutch harbor.

Among the passengers on the ships were ten refugee families from Spain. They appeared to be Spanish noblemen, but actually they were Marranos—secret Jews, who remained loyal to their faith despite the persecutions of the Inquisition. To all appearances they were Christians, but in secret they observed their Jewish faith and festivals. Life in Spain, however, was made impossible for them, for the agents of the dreaded Inquisition watched them constantly, and anyone suspected of practising any Jewish precept was burnt alive at the stake, and his wealth was forfeited to the Church. And so these ten families had hired ships and fled from Spain in search of a friendly country, where they would be able to throw off their hateful disguise and become Jews openly and freely. Divine Providence brought them to the shores of Holland, which, not long before, had freed herself from Spanish domination.

These Jewish families were among the noblest and richest in Castilia (Spain). They were fortunate to be able to take with them a great deal of their possessions, gold, silver, household goods and merchandise.

While the ships were undergoing repairs, the Marranos took their possessions off the ships, and rented rooms in the harbor. After a good night's rest, one of the passengers with his son, took a walk in the street. They passed a butcher store, where a fine duck was hanging in the window, with a label on which there were two

Hebrew words: בשר כשר. The boy had never seen such writing before. "What strange language is this?" He asked his father.

"Hush!" his father replied, and the boy wondered why his father's face suddenly grew pale.

They went right back, and the father asked the innkeeper, "Are there any Jews in this place, and are they allowed to live in peace?"

"Yes, señor," replied the innkeeper. "Since our country threw off the yoke of your country twelve years ago, in 1581, this has become a free country, where any one can live in peace and worship his G-d according to his faith."

This was wonderful news, and the señor continued to ask the innkeeper if there was a Rabbi in that community, and could he perhaps introduce him to the Rabbi?

"Certainly, señor. I will be glad to take you to the Rabbi. He is a fine gentleman, beloved by all. His name is Rabbi Moshe Uri," the innkeeper said.

Two elders of the Marranos lost no time and went to see the Rabbi.

Rabbi Moshe Uri Ashkenazi had come from Germany ("Ashkenazi" means "The German"), and the little Jewish community in the Dutch harbor town welcomed him and honored him for his learning and kindness to all. When the two Spanish noblemen came to him, he received them in a very friendly way, but he could not understand their language. His son Aaron served as interpreter.

"We have confidential business to discuss with you," the Spanish gentlemen said, throwing a suspicious glance at the young man.

"You may speak freely, gentlemen," the Rabbi replied, "for this is my son Aaron."

The two Marranos told the Rabbi who they were,

and how they chanced to come to this town. "We want to return to our faith and be reunited with our people. For many years we have risked our lives to remain loyal to our G-d and our Torah, but we were not able to do very much under the watchful eyes of the Inquisition. Most of us are ignorant of the Torah; we are uncircumcised; our children do not even know the Aleph-Beth. But the fire of devotion to G-d still burns in our hearts. Help us, Rabbi, to return to our people."

Rabbi Moshe Uri listened to their story which had moved him to tears. When they finished their tale of horror of what they had been through under the shadow of the Inquisition, the Rabbi replied, "My dear brethren, in this place it would not be advisable for you to stay. There are very few Jews here, and your arrival has already created a stir in town. The country people are suspicious of Spaniards and we might all get into trouble. However, the city of Amsterdam is not far away. There is a larger Jewish community there. Go to Amsterdam, and rent rooms in Junkerstraat, and hang out a red ribbon from the window. In a few days from now, we will come and circumcise all your men and boys to bring you into the Covenant of our father Abraham. Then we will teach you all you have to know about our faith, and you will live with us like brothers."

The Marranos followed the Rabbi's advice. In due course, Rabbi Moshe Uri and his son Aaron arrived in Amsterdam and went to Junkerstraat. Soon they were embraced affectionately by the Marranos. The *Brith* (circumcision) took place quietly. The first to enter the Covenant of our father Abraham was Don Jacob Tirado, the oldest and noblest of them all. Then one by one they were all circumcised. After they recuperated, Rabbi Moshe Uri and his son began to teach them all that Jews have to know about their faith, how to pray from the Siddur, say the blessings, put on Tefillin, and so on, and the Spanish Jews learnt with diligence and devotion, until they needed the services of Rabbi Moshe Uri no longer. They sent word to their Spanish brethren, relatives and friends, secretly informing them how fortunate they were to be in Holland, and urging them to join them. Thus the little Spanish Jewish community grew, under the leadership of Don Jacob Tirado. They lived quietly, trying not to attract too much attention, as the fear of the Inquisition was still very strong in their hearts.

Then came the Solemn Days of Rosh Hashanah, and Yom Kippur. The Day of Atonement was always observed by the Marranos in Spain. They used to gather in the cellars of their homes to pray to G-d on this most solemn day of the year. Now, being in free Holland, it was not necessary for them to do so in secret, but they were still frightened in case the long arms of the Inquisition might reach even here. So they locked the doors of their synagogue and prayed to G-d as never before.

Now the neighbors who had noticed many Spaniards gather in one place behind locked doors, with strange sounds coming from inside, grew suspicious. They notified the Governor of the city of the secret meeting, where they were sure a plot was being made against the free country of Holland, in order to recapture it for the king of Spain.

The Governor himself led a platoon of soldiers to Junkerstraat. He knocked at the locked doors: "Open in the name of the Law!"

The worshippers nearly died of fright. Somebody shouted, "The Inquisition is here!" and a terrible panic broke out among the frightened worshippers, who began to jump out of the windows to escape, but most of them were rounded up and captured.

Only the venerable Jacob Tirado remained fearless

to face the intruders. The soldiers searched the place for weapons, but found nothing but prayerbooks and *Talleithim.*

"Who are you? And what are you doing in this place so secretly?" the Governor demanded to know.

Still unable to speak Dutch, Don Jacob Tirado addressed the Governor in Latin. He told him who they were: how they had escaped from the terrible Inquisition, and would never wish to see it spread its ugly wings over this peaceful and free state. He told him further that it was the holiest day for the Jews, the Day of Atonement, and they had gathered to pray to G-d. But the fear of the Inquisition was so strong in their hearts that they still gathered to pray in secret. Don Jacob Tirado further told the Governor that they were useful and peaceful citizens, that they would not be a public charge, but rather the contrary, for they had brought their wealth with them and were already developing trade and commerce for the good of the country.

The Governor was greatly impressed by the words of Jacob Tirado. He shook his hand, assured him that they were welcome, and more like them would be welcome in free Holland. "You may worship your G-d here in freedom, and without fear. Pray also for us," he said as he took his leave with a friendly smile.

It was a great day for the young community of the Spanish Jews in Amsterdam. At last they were rid of their fear. Soon they built a real synagogue, which bore the name "Beth Jacob" after their beloved leader, Jacob Tirado. One of the first Rabbis of the growing community of Spanish and Portuguese Jews in Amsterdam was the famous Rabbi Manasseh ben Israel.*

---

* 5364-5417 after Creation.

THE PRINCESS

(A parable by the famous Preacher of Dubno)

Once upon a time there lived a great king, who had an only daughter. The princess was noble and fair, and when she grew up, the king looked for a worthy young man to be his daughter's husband. Many dukes and princes wooed the royal princess, but she turned them down one after another. "This one is a glutton," she said, and "that one is too fond of wine." The king became impatient, and swore that the next young man that would come to the gates of the palace would be the princess' husband.

It so happened that the next man to come to the palace gates was a simple peasant. But true to his word, the King married off his daughter to the peasant. The bridegroom took his bride to his village, where he set up his home. To the peasant, the princess was just a wife, and he treated her as he had always thought he would treat his wife. She worked hard, until her pretty face and hands became rough from toil. The villagers often made fun of her and insulted her.

The poor princess was very unhappy. She began writing to her father every day, bitterly complaining to him about her lot. The king felt sorry for his beloved daughter, and sent word to her that on a certain day he would come to visit her. The news soon spread through the village that the king was coming to visit his daughter, and there was a great to-do. Everybody came to the house of the king's son-in-law to help scrub and clean up the place, and decorate it. The king's daughter was now treated with great respect. No more dirty work for her. She was given a beauty treatment and dressed up in fine clothes. Everybody was very friendly and respectful to her.

The time came when the king's runner came dashing

into the village, bringing news that the king was on his way, approaching the village. Everybody turned out to greet the king. "Long live the King!" "Long live the Princess!" they shouted, as they accompanied the king and his daughter into the decorated and illuminated village. The king entered the home of his son-in-law and found it clean and spotless, and decorated with bunting and flowers. He saw the great honor and respect which his daughter enjoyed and he was pleased. He wondered why his daughter had been sending him such alarming letters. Father and daughter spent a happy day together, and the king then prepared to take his leave. The princess embraced her father and cried bitterly, "O father, dear father, don't leave me here; take me with you! Please, take me back home!"

"But my dear daughter," the king replied, "you seem to be happy here; the way they seem to treat you here, I am sure no princess has enjoyed more honor and affection."

"O, dear father," the princess cried, "all this honor and affection they showed me today is for your benefit. They heard you were coming, so they made a big fuss about me. But the moment you leave, they will begin to treat me as before, insult me, and make me very unhappy."

The king called his son-in-law to his side, and asked him, "Is this the way to treat my daughter? Don't you know that she is a princess?"

The husband's eyes were filled with tears, as he replied, "Your Majesty, I know she is a princess, but what can I do? I am a poor man, I must work very hard for a living. I am unable to give her the kind of life she really deserves. Besides, I live in a village, among people full of wickedness and envy. They do not appreciate your daughter's qualities, and take every opportunity to insult her. But you are a great king. Since you found it wise to take me for a son-in-law, take me away from here; lift me up to your position; give me an estate worthy of your daughter and of the king's son-in-law, and I will then be able to give your daughter the kind of life she really deserves!"

* * *

The King of Kings, the Holy One, Blessed be He, wanted to give his daughter—the Torah—to Adam, the first man, whom G-d created with His own hands. But the Torah said, "He is a glutton; he ate of the Tree of Knowledge against your express command." Then G-d wished to give the Torah to Noah, and the Torah said, "He is too fond of wine; did he not plant a vineyard and did he not get drunk?" Finally G-d gave the Torah to the children of Israel, whom He had just brought out of Egyptian bondage.

All year round the Torah is often neglected and even shamed. Day after day the Torah sends a message to the king, complaining about her treatment, as it is written, "Every day a heavenly voice calls out, 'Woe to the creatures for shaming the Torah!' "

Then come the king's messengers to announce the arrival of the king—they are the days of Elul heralding the coming of Rosh Hashanah. We then wake up, and begin feverish preparations; we pray and learn and recite Psalms, as never before. Rosh Hashanah does not find us unprepared. We sound the Shofar and hail the King of Kings. G-d is among us, and we enjoy His Divine light, and our hearts are filled with the nearness of G-d, with reverence and love for His Divine Majesty.

Yom Kippur comes, and G-d finds all Jews repenting, pure and holy, like angels. But after *Ne'ilah* is over and the Shofar is sounded to announce the departure of the *Shechinah*, the Torah begins to cry, "Father, father, don't leave me! Take me with you, for soon they will take away all the glory from me, and forget who I am, and mistreat me again!"

Then G-d says to His people, "Is this the way to treat my daughter? Don't you know that the Torah is a Divine princess!" And the Jewish people answers, "Master of the Universe! Indeed, we know the greatness of the Torah. But what can we do? We live in poverty, and have no proper home. We live among the nations of the world, who do not want to know about the Torah. So please take us away from here; take us back to our holy land, for all the world is yours; give us back our holy land as an inheritance, and we shall be able to keep the Torah in glory!"

That is why we pray, immediately after the Shofar is sounded on the night of Yom Kippur, "Next year in Jerusalem, through our Righteous Messiah, and there we shall serve Thee as in the days of old!"

DID YOU KNOW?

The first day of Rosh-Hashanah cannot ever occur on Sunday, Wednesday or Friday.

* * *

The New Moon of Tishrei is not announced nor is it blessed in the Synagogue on the Sabbath preceding it, as in the case of all other months. G-d Himself blesses this month.

* * *

Adam was created on the first day of Tishrei (Rosh-Hashanah), and He immediately proclaimed the Creator as the King and Master of the Universe. This is one of the reasons why the Shofar is sounded on Rosh-Hashanah.

* * *

Because Rosh-Hashanah is the "Coronation Day" of the King of Kings, the Holy One, Blessed be He, it is a day of amnesty and forgiveness.

* * *

The Shofar is also a call to repentance. The first man to repent was Cain who slew his brother Abel on this day. He repented, and his life was spared.

* * *

There is an opinion to the effect that Isaac was born on Rosh-Hashanah, and that is why we read in the Torah about his birth on the first day of Rosh-Hashanah, and about the Binding of Isaac (*Akedah*) on the second.

* * *

It was on Rosh-Hashanah when Joseph was freed from prison in Egypt, and became Viceroy of Egypt.

* * *

Ezra the Scribe gathered all the returning exiles from Babylon on the day of Rosh-Hashanah, and together with the prophet Nehemiah roused them to passionate repentance and devotion to G-d.

* * *

When the first day of Rosh-Hashanah occurs on the Sabbath, *Tashlich* is observed on the second day.

* * *

The white gown (*Kittel*) worn on the Day of Atonement is symbolic of purity from sin, for on that day we are likened to angels: we do not eat, nor drink, but pray all the time, and are free from sin.

* * *

At Minchah on Yom-Kippur we read from the Book of Jonah, where we learn about the greatness of Teshuvah (repentance), how G-d is always ready to forgive the sinner if he returns to G-d sincerely.

* * *

During the Yom-Kippur service in the Beth Hamikdosh of old, the High Priest changed his garments five times in the following order: Golden garments, linen garments, golden, linen, and golden garments again.

* * *

At the end of the Yom-Kippur services the Shofar is sounded for various reasons:

It is a reminder of the Shofar which used to be sounded on Yom-Kippur to announce the year of Jubilee (Lev. 25).

It is a symbol of victory, as the sounding of trumpets by a victorious army returning from the field. The Shofar sounds the victory over our sins and temptations.

It is also a reminder of the receiving of the Second Tablets, for on Yom Kippur Moses came down for the last time from Mount Sinai, bearing the Second Tablets with the Ten Commandments, which the children of Israel received with joy, and welcomed with the sounding of the Shofar.

Another significant reason for the sounding of the Shofar at the end of the Yom Kippur services is that it is a sign of the departure of the *Shechinah,* as it is written, "G-d has ascended with the sound of the Shofar" (Ps. 47).

* * *

It is written in the Midrash, that at the termination of the Yom Kippur fast, a Heavenly voice calls out, "Go eat thy bread with joy, for G-d accepted thy prayers and has forgiven thee!" It is therefore a Yom Tov and we greet each other with "Good Yomtov." The sounding of the Shofar serves also to call attention to the importance of this Yom-Tov.

* * *

After sounding of the Shofar at the end of the *Ne'ilah* Services on Yom Kippur we call out *Leshono habo'o biRusholaim*—Next year may we be in Jerusalem. On two occasions in the year we call out, "Next year in Jerusalem": On the night of Yom Kippur, and on the night of the Seder. In the Talmud (*Rosh Hashanah,* 11a) there are two opinions regarding the *Ge'ulah* (Redemption): One opinion holds that in the month of Nissan the Jews were redeemed from Egypt, and in the month of Nissan they will be redeemed in the future through our Righteous Messiah. The other opinion holds that we were redeemed from Egypt in the month of Nissan, but the future Redemption will be in the month of Tishrei. That is why on both occasions, in Nissan (Pesach) as well as in Tishrei (Yom Kippur) we exclaim, *Leshono habo'o biYerusholaim!*

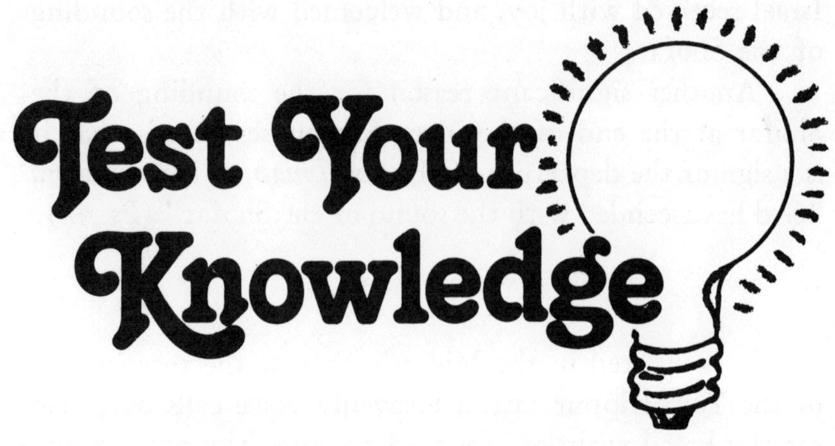

One of the three answers is right

ANSWERS ON PAGE 222

A.

ROSH HASHANAH

1. With the month of Elul begins a period of special Divine grace, lasting: (a) Ten days; (b) Fifteen days; (c) Forty days?
2. During the month of Elul the Shofar is (a) sounded without a blessing; (b) sounded with a blessing; (c) not sounded at all?
3. Tishrei is (a) the first month of the year; (b) the third month of the year; (c) the seventh month of the year?
4. The first day of Rosh Hashanah is (a) the first day of the incoming year; (b) the last day of the outgoing year; (c) the middle of the year?
5. The first day of Rosh Hashanah cannot be on (a) Sunday, Tuesday and Thursday; (b) Sunday, Wednesday and Friday; (c) Monday, Wednesday and Friday?
6. The Shofar is sounded on each day of Rosh Hashanah: (a) 30 times; (b) 90 times; (c) 100 times?
7. If the first day of Rosh Hashanah is on Sabbath, the Shofar is sounded (a) on the first day only; (b) on the second day only; (c) on both days equally?

8. Tashlich is usually observed on the first day of Rosh Hashanah, unless it is: (a) Friday; (b) Sabbath; (c) Sunday?
9. How many scrolls are taken from the Ark for the reading in the Torah on Rosh Hashanah: (a) One; (b) Two; (c) Three?
10. How many people are called up to the reading in the Torah on Rosh Hashanah not counting *Maftir*: (a) Five on week-days and seven on Sabbath; (b) Six on week-days and seven on Sabbath; (c) Seven on both week-days and Sabbath?
11. The Haphtorah read on the first day of Rosh Hashanah is about the birth of the prophet (a) Samuel; (b) Jonah; (c) Micah?
12. The Haphtorah of the first day of Rosh Hashanah contains a famous "song" by the prophetess: (a) Miriam; (b) Deborah; (c) Hannah?
13. The prophet Samuel belonged to the tribe of: (a) Judah; (b) Levi; (c) Ephraim?
14. On Rosh Hashanah we say: (a) All the Hallel; (b) Half Hallel; (c) No Hallel?

B.

BETWEEN ROSH HASHANAH AND YOM-KIPPUR

15. The Fast of Gedaliah is observed on: (a) the third day of Tishrei; (b) the fifth day of Tishrei; (c) the 15th day of Tishrei?
16. Gedaliah was: (a) leader of a Jewish revolt against the Romans; (b) a governor appointed by Nebuchadnezzar; (c) the last king of Judah?
17. If the Fast of Gedaliah occurs on the Sabbath it is observed (a) on Sunday; (b) Friday; (c) Thursday?
18. The Ten Days of Repentance: (a) include Rosh Hashanah and Yom Kippur; (b) do not include Rosh Hashanah and Yom Kippur; (c) include Yom Kippur, but not Rosh Hashanah?
19. "Shabbos-Shuvah" is so called: (a) after the first word of the Haphtorah; (b) after the first word of the Sidrah; (c) after the name of a prophet?
20. The Haphtorah on Shabbos-Shuvah is taken from the book of: (a) Isaiah; (b) Hosea; (c) Micah?

C.

YOM KIPPUR

Match the following

1.	From Rosh Chodesh Elul to Yom Kippur: —	a.	*Al-chet*
2.	Yom Kippur night: —	b.	Whale
3.	Forbidden leather footwear: —	c.	Forty Days' Divine grace
4.	The Long Confession: —	d.	Neilah
5.	Jonah: —	e.	One blast of the Shofar
6.	Closing prayer of Yom Kippur: —	f.	Kiddush-Levanah
7.	After Neilah: —	g.	Kol Nidrei
8.	After Maariv at the termination of the fast: —	h.	One of the "Five Afflictions" on Yom-Kippur

(*Answers on Page* 222)

SUCCOTH

SUCCOTH

The Festival of Tabernacles

A joyful period is ushered in by the festival of Succoth which compensates for the solemn period of the *Yamim Noraim.* Succoth is "the season of our rejoicing." On Succoth we have a Mitzvah that is truly unique, for the Succah is the only Mitzvah that literally encompasses us, as we walk into it.

The Succah reminds us of the "Clouds of Glory" that surrounded our people during their wandering through the desert on the way to the Promised Land. Everybody then saw the special Divine protection that G-d bestowed upon them during those difficult years. But although the "Clouds of Glory" disappeared in the fortieth year, on the eve of their entry into the Land of Israel, we have never ceased to believe that G-d gives us His own protection, and that is why we have outlived our greatest enemies in all generations. We know of course that we enjoy this divine protection only as long as we remain loyal Jews, faithful to our G-d and our Torah. This explains why we have *Simchath Torah* (rejoicing with our Torah) at the end of the Succoth festival. But about this day later.

The Four Kinds

One of the special Succoth Mitzvoth is the Mitzvah of the "Four Kinds" — the Lulav, Ethrog, Myrtle and Weeping Willow. This is a Mitzvah like any other Mitzvah of the Torah, but it is a very significant one and symbolic of unity and harmony. When the blessings are recited over them, it is customary to wave them to all the four winds and also upward and downward, signifying that G-d is everywhere.

The traditional prayer "Hoshana" (O save!) which is said on each of the days of Succoth (except Shabbos), is accompanied by a procession with the "Four Kinds" around the *Bimah* in the *Shul*. It makes a beautiful and impressive sight. One can just imagine how in the days of old thousands upon thousands of Jewish pilgrims marched to the Holy Temple with Lulavim in their hands swaying with the breeze. It is told that on one occasion, when the king, who also held the office of High Priest at that time, displayed his leaning for reform by performing a certain ritual in the Temple not in the traditional way, thousands of *Ethrogim* rained down upon him from the displeased worshippers!

Hoshana-Rabba

The seventh day of Succoth is called *Hoshana-Rabba* (Great Hoshana).

On the night of *Hoshana-Rabba* it is customary to stay awake, reciting the *Tikkun* and Psalms.

During the morning service of Hoshana-Rabba, after the Hoshana prayers, having marched with the Lulav seven times around the *Bimah*, the "Four Kinds" are put away, and the "Hoshanas" (willow-branches) are taken in their stead, and beaten upon the floor, while saying a special prayer.

THE CELEBRATION OF WATER-DRAWING

(*From the Mishnah, Succah* 5)

What was the manner of the *Water-Libation?* They used to fill a golden flagon holding three *logs** with water drawn from the Siloam. When they reached the Water Gate they blew on the Shofar a *tekiah - teruah - tekiah.* On the right of the Altar Ramp were two silver bowls. They each had a hole like a narrow snout — one wide, the other narrow — so that both bowls emptied themselves together (the wider one was for wine, since wine flows out more slowly). The bowl to the west was for water and the one to the east was for wine.

He that never has seen the *Simchath Beth Hashoevah* (the Joy of the Water-Drawing) has never in his life seen joy.

At the close of the first Festival-day they went down to the Court of the Women,** and made great preparations there.

There were golden candlesticks there with four golden bowls on the top of them. The candlesticks were fifty cubits high. Four ladders led up to each candlestick, and four youths from the priestly stock went up holding in their hands jars of oil, of twenty-four *logs'* capacity, which they poured into the bowls.

They made wicks out of worn-out garments of the

---

*) A log is about ½ a pint.

**) The Court of the Women (*Ezrath Nashim*) was one hundred and thirty-five cubits long and one hundred and thirty-five cubits wide. At its four corners were four roofless chambers, each of forty cubits. Fifteen steps led up from the Court of the Women to the Court of the (male) Israelites, corresponding to the fifteen Songs of Ascents (*Shir HaMaaloth*) in the Psalms (120-134), and upon them the Levites used to sing.

priests, and with them they set the candlesticks alight, and there was not a courtyard in Jerusalem that did not reflect the light of the *Beth-Hashoevah.*

Men of piety and good deeds used to dance before them with burning torches in their hands, singing songs and praises. And countless Levites played on harps, lyres, cymbals and trumpets and other instruments of music, on the fifteen steps leading from the Court of the Israelites to the Court of the Women. Two priests stood at the Upper Gate,*) which leads down from the Court of the Israelites to the Court of the Women, with two trumpets in their hands. At cock-crow they blew a *tekiah-teruah-tekiah.* When they reached the tenth step, they again blew a *tekiah-teruah-tekiah.* When they reached the Court they again blew a *tekiah-teruah-tekiah.* They went on until they reached the gate that leads out to the east. When they reached that gate, they turned their faces toward the west (facing the Sanctuary). . . Rabbi Judah said, "They used to repeat the words, 'We belong to G-d, and our eyes are turned to G-d.' "

* * *

It was related of Old Hillel that when he was rejoicing with the joy of the Water-Drawing, he used to say, ". . . Where I love to be, thither my legs carry me." And the Holy One, blessed is He, says, "If you come to My house, I will come to your house, and if you do not come to My house, neither will I come to yours."

It was related of Rabban Shimon ben Gamliel that when he was rejoicing with the Joy of the Water-Drawing he would take eight burning torches in one hand and toss them upwards; he tossed one and caught one, and never did one touch the other. . . . (*T.B. Succah* 53).

---

*) The famous *Nicanor Gate.*

THE FESTIVAL OF INGATHERING

Succoth is the Festival of Ingathering; it is the time when the produce of the field, orchard and vineyard is gathered in. The granaries, threshing floors and wine- and olive-presses are full to capacity. Weeks and months of toil and sweat put into the soil have finally been amply rewarded. The farmer feels happy and elated. No wonder Succoth is "the Season of Rejoicing."

At such a time of material success, there is the danger of man "waxing fat and kicking; forsaking G-d, his Maker." Finding his work so successfully rewarded, he may think that "my power and the strength of my hand have made me all this wealth." There is also the danger of his thinking that to work and amass a fortune is the whole purpose of life, forgetting that there are greater and higher values in life—spiritual values.

Lest the Jew forget his real purpose in life, G-d, in His infinite wisdom and loving-kindness, bade us leave our comfortable homes at this time, and dwell in a frail Succah for seven days. The Succah reminds us that we rely on G-d for protection, for the Succah is no fortress, not even providing a solid roof over our heads. It reminds us also that life on this earth is but a temporary dwelling. The seven days of Succoth, each represent a decade of life, seventy years in all, the human life-span on this earth. This short life-span should be considered only as a period of preparation for the everlasting life that comes *after* life on this earth, a life where material wealth does not count, where only spiritual wealth counts. The stores of grain, wine and oil must be left behind, while only the stores of Torah, Mitzvoth and Good Deeds can be taken along and put to good advantage in that everlasting life.

This is also one of the reasons why it is customary, in some congregations, to read the Book of Ecclesiastes

(*Koheleth*) during the Festival of Succoth. In some congregations it is read in the synagogue on Shabbos Chol-Hamoed Succoth. For the Book of Koheleth, prophetically written by the Wisest of All men, King Solomon, is full of earnest thoughts and reflections on the "vanity of vanities" of this world. It fittingly concludes with the words, "The end of the matter after all is heard, is: Fear G-d and keep His commandments, for this is the whole purpose of man."

In this way, Succoth for us is the "Festival of Ingathering" in a deeper sense: it teaches us to gather, retain and store up the religious experiences and spiritual uplift which we have acquired during the many and varied festivals, prayers and Mitzvoth of the month of Tishrei, so that we can draw upon these rich stores throughout the whole year to come.

SELECTIONS FROM MIDRASH ON KOHELETH

The Wise Choice

Rabbi Simon related in the name of Rabbi Shimeon ben Halafta the following parable:

A great king had a friend and counsellor who was a very wise man. One day the king said to his friend, "I want to give you a present; ask anything you desire."

The wise man thought, "What shall I ask of the king? Shall I ask for gold and silver and precious stones? He will surely give them to me. Shall I ask for beautiful robes and clothes? He will surely give them to me. I will rather ask his daughter's hand in marriage; then I will surely have everything."

So with King Solomon. In the town of Gibeon, G-d appeared unto him in a dream and said to him, "Ask anything of Me, and I will give it to you." The wise King Solomon thought, "Shall I ask for silver, gold and precious stones? G-d will surely give them to me. I will rather ask for *wisdom,* then I will have everything." And Solomon replied to G-d, "Give Thy servant an understanding and wise heart." Said G-d to Solomon, "Because you asked for wisdom, but did not ask for riches, or honor, or victory over your enemies—I will give you wisdom and knowledge, and riches and honor as well."

When Solomon awoke from his sleep, he knew that it was a dream, but he soon realized that the dream came true, for he heard a bird twitter, and he understood its language, and he heard a donkey bray, and he knew what the donkey wanted. King Solomon became the wisest of all men. He went to Jerusalem, and prayed before the Ark of G-d, and he offered sacrifices, and made a great feast of thanksgiving. The spirit of prophecy rested on him, and he composed the three holy books of the Scriptures: *Mishlei* (Proverbs), *Shir-haShirim* (Song of Songs) and *Koheleth* (Ecclesiastes).

Under the Sun and Above the Sun

"What profit hath man of all his labor wherein he laboreth under the sun" (Koheleth 1:3).

"Of all *his* labor"—all that man labors for his own benefit, for his worldly pleasures—man has no profit. But of the labor he labors for his soul, his efforts for Torah, Mitzvoth and good deeds, for himself *and* others—of that he has a lasting profit.

Rabbi Huna and Rabbi Aha taught in the name of Rabbi Halafta:

"*Under* the sun"—all man's labors for something which is *under* the sun, all worldly gains and profits—are of no profit; but *above* the sun—efforts for Torah and Mitzvoth, which are above everything—are of lasting profit.

SUNSET AND SUNRISE

"The sun rises, and the sun goes down" (Koheleth 1:5).

Said Rabbi Berechiah, "Do we not know that the sun rises and sets? But Koheleth teaches here that before the sun of one spiritual leader goes down, the sun of his successor already rises. On the day Rabbi Akiba died, Rabbi Judah the Prince was born. Before the sun of our Mother Sarah went down, the sun of our Mother Rebeckah had risen. Before the sun of Moses set, the sun of Joshua had risen. And so it is in every generation: before the spiritual leader passes away, Divine Providence provides another to take his place.

THE OCEAN IS NEVER FILLED

"All the rivers run into the sea, yet the sea is not full" (Koheleth 1:7).

The Torah is likened to water, without which man cannot exist. All the Torah that one learns goes into one's heart, but the heart cannot be filled, for the Divine Soul is never sated with Torah; it always thirsts for more and more.

Never be afraid of losing any Torah by teaching it to others. For just as the ocean never loses its water, since it always comes back to it, so the Torah you teach to others will not make you poorer; rather the opposite, it will come back to you as sweet water of the rivers.

Trial and Answer

"That is an evil thing which G-d hath given to man to be answered (also: afflicted) by it" (Koheleth 1:13).

"That" refers to money and riches, which are sometimes a blessing and sometimes, G-d forbid, a curse.

Rabbi Judah said in the name of Rabbi Levi: When a man merits it, and uses his money for doing Mitzvoth and good deeds, his prayers will be answered. But if he does not use his money for good purposes, it will appear as testimony against him.

(This is a play on the Hebrew verb *la'anoth,* used in the text, which has three meanings: to *answer,* to *afflict,* to *give testimony*).

Crooked that Cannot Be Made Straight

"That which is crooked cannot be made straight" (Koheleth 1:15).

In this life, one whose path has become crooked, straying from the right path of the Torah, can straighten it through *Teshuvah,* Repentance. But in the world to come, the crooked cannot be straightened, and failures cannot be made good; it is too late then.

Two wicked men who were close friends and partners in crime, died. One of them was received among the righteous; the other among the wicked. The latter looked in vain for his friend, and then saw him from a distance, enjoying the Divine Light among the righteous. "Hey, brother, how do you come to be there?" the wicked man called out. Then he protested, "Is there bribery in *this* World of Truth? We were partners in crime during our life on earth; now I see him among the righteous over there, while I have to languish here among the wicked! Is this what you call justice?"

The answer stunned him: "You fool! Your friend

had sense enough to do penitence before he died; he turned away from his evil ways, and went straight for the rest of his life."

"Let me repent, too!" cried the sinner.

What he hears in reply, crushes him with grief: "You fool! Don't you know that this world is called 'Shabbos' while the world you came from is called 'Erev-Shabbos?' If you do not prepare anything on Erev-Shabbos, what will you eat on Shabbos? Don't you know that this world is called 'Sea' while the world you came from is called 'Land?' If a man sets out on a sea-voyage without preparing himself while on dry land, what is he going to do at sea? Don't you know that this world is called 'Desert' while the world you came from is 'inhabited?' If a man does not prepare himself for the journey in the desert, while still in an inhabited country, what can he do in the desert? Don't you know that this world is called 'Winter' while the world you came from is called 'Summer?' If you do not plough, sow and reap during the summer, what will you eat in the winter?"

The Whole Purpose of Man

"The end of the matter, after all is heard: Fear G-d and keep His commandments, for this is the whole purpose of man" (Koheleth 12:13).

"Fear G-d"—refers to all the prohibitions, the sins which one must not do; they are 365 in number.

"Keep His commandments"—refers to the positive commandments, which one must do; they are 248 in number.

Together there are 613 commandments in the Torah (*Taryag*), which are the duty of the Jew to fulfill, and his purpose in life. In doing this, he is happy in this world, and happy also in the Everlasting World.

THE FOX AND THE VINEYARD

King Solomon, the wisest of all men, reminds us to be very humble, for as man comes into this world with nothing, so does he leave with no riches.

Our Sages give us the following parable, in order that these wise words of Solomon should remain fresh in our memory:

A sly fox passed a lovely vineyard. A tall, thick fence surrounded the vineyard on all sides. As the fox circled around the fence, he found a small hole in the fence, barely large enough for him to push his head through. The fox could see what luscious grapes grew in the vineyard, and his mouth began to water. But the hole was too small for him.

So what did the sly fox do? He fasted for three days until he became so thin that he managed to slip through the hole.

Inside the vineyard the fox began to eat to his heart's content. He grew bigger and fatter than ever before. Then he wanted to get out of the vineyard. But alas! The hole was too small again. So what did he do? He fasted for three days again, and then just about managed to slip through the hole and out again.

Turning his head towards the vineyard, the poor fox said: "Vineyard, O vineyard! How lovely you look, and how lovely are your fruits and vines. But what good are you to me? Just as I came to you, so I leave you. . . ."

And so, our Sages say, it is also with this world. It is a beautiful world, but just as man comes into this world empty-handed, so he leaves it. Only the Torah he studied, the Mitzvoth he performed, and the good deeds he practiced are the real fruits which he can take with him.

AN ETHROG FROM THE GARDEN OF EDEN

It was the first day of Succoth, and all the congregants in the "Shul" of Rabbi Elimelech of Lisensk were in a festive mood. One could feel the "Yom-Tov" spirit in the atmosphere.

As Rabbi Elimelech stood at the "Amud" and began reciting "Hallel," all eyes turned upon him. There was something unusual in his manner this Succoth. Why did he stop so suddenly in the middle of his swaying as he held the "Ethrog" and "Lulav" in his hands to sniff the air? And why did he not go through the Service in his usual leisurely manner? It was evident that something was on his mind, something rather exciting by the look on his radiant countenance!

The minute the "davvening" was over, Rabbi Elimelech hurried to where his brother Rabbi Zusia (who had come to spend Yom-Tov with him) was standing, and said to him eagerly: "Come and help me find the 'Ethrog' which is permeating the whole 'Shul' with the fragrance of the Garden of Eden!"

And so together they went from person to person until they reached the far corner of the "Shul" where a quiet-looking individual was standing, obviously engrossed in his own thoughts.

"This is the one," called out Rabbi Elimelech delightedly. "Please, dear friend, tell me who are you and where you obtained this wonderful 'Ethrog'?"

The man, looking somewhat startled and bewildered at this unexpected question, replied rather slowly, carefully choosing his words:

"With all due respect to you, Rabbi, it is quite a story. Do you wish to sit down and listen to it all?"

"Most certainly I do," answered Rabbi Elimelech emphatically, "I am sure it will be a story worth hearing!"

"My name," began the quiet-looking man, "is Uri, and I come from Strelisk. I have always regarded 'Ethrog-Bentschen' as one of my favorite 'Mitzvoth,' and so, although I am a poor man and could normally not afford to buy an 'Ethrog' according to my desire, my young wife, who agrees with me as to its importance, helps me by hiring herself out as cook. Thus she is independent of any financial help from me, and I can use my own earnings for spiritual matters. I am employed as 'Melamed' (teacher) in the village of Yanev, which is not far from my native town. One half of my earnings I use for our needs and with the other half I buy an 'Ethrog' in Lemberg. But in order not to spend any money on the journey I usually go on foot.

"This year, during the 'Ten Days of Repentance,' I was making my way on foot as usual, with fifty gulden in my wallet with which to buy an 'Ethrog,' when on the road to Lemberg I passed through a forest and stopped at a wayside inn to have a rest. It was time for 'Minchah' so I stood in a corner and 'davvened' Minchah.

"I was in the middle of 'Shemone-Esrei' when I heard a terrible sound of moaning and groaning, as of one in great anguish. I hurriedly finished my 'davvening' so that I could find out what was the trouble, and if I could help in any way.

"As I turned towards the man who was in obvious distress, I beheld a most unusual and rough looking person, dressed in peasant garb with a whip in his hands, pouring out his troubles to the inn-keeper at the bar.

"From the somewhat confused story, between his sobs, I managed to gather that the man with the whip was a poor Jew who earned his living as a 'Baal-Agallah' (owner of a horse and cart for carting purposes). He had a wife and several children and he barely managed to earn enough to make ends meet. And now, a terrible calamity had befallen him. His horse, without which he could do nothing, had suddenly collapsed in the forest not far from the inn, and just lay there unable to get up.

"I could not bear to see the man's despair and tried to encourage him, by telling him that he must not forget that there is a G-d above us who could help him in his trouble, however serious it seemed to him.

" 'I'll sell you another horse for fifty gulden, although I assure you he is worth at least eighty, but just to help you out in your difficulty!' " The inn-keeper was saying to the 'Baal-Agallah.'

" 'I haven't even fifty cents, and he tells me I can buy a horse for fifty gulden!' the man said bitterly.

"I felt I could not keep the money I had with me for an 'Ethrog' when here was a man in such desperate plight that his very life and that of his family depended upon his getting a horse. So I said to the inn-keeper:

" 'Tell me what is the lowest price you would take for your horse?'

"The inn-keeper turned to me in surprise. 'If you pay me cash down, I will take forty-five gulden, but absolutely not a cent less. I am selling my horse at a loss as it is!'

"I immediately took out my wallet and handed him forty-five gulden, the 'Baal-Agallah' looking on, his eyes nearly bulging out of their sockets in astonishment. He was just speechless with relief, and his joy was absolutely indescribable!

" 'Now you see that the Almighty *can* help you, even when the position appears to you to be entirely hopeless!' I said to him as he hurried off with the inn-keeper to harness the newly-bought horse to his forsaken cart tied to the stricken horse in the forest.

"As soon as they went off, I hurriedly got my few things together and disappeared, as I did not want to be embarrassed by the thanks of the grateful 'Baal-Agallah'.

"I eventually reached Lemberg with the remaining five gulden in my pocket, and naturally had to content myself with buying a very ordinary looking but kosher 'Ethrog!' My original intention had been to spend fifty gulden for an 'Ethrog' as I do every year, but as you have heard, I decided that the need of the 'Baal-Agallah' for a horse was greater than my need for an 'exceptional Ethrog.'

"Usually my 'Ethrog' is the best in Yanev, and everyone used to come and 'bentsch' with it, but this year I was ashamed to return home with such a poor-looking specimen, so my wife agreed that I could come here to Lisensk, where nobody knew me."

"But my dear Rabbi Uri," cried out Rabbi Elimelech, now that the former had finished his story, "Yours is indeed an exceptional 'Ethrog!' Now I realize why your 'Ethrog' has the fragrance of the Garden of Eden in its perfume! Let me tell you the sequel to your story!"

"When the 'Baal-Agallah' whom you saved, thought about his unexpected good fortune, he decided that you must have been none other than the Prophet Elijah whom the Almighty had sent down to earth in the form of a man, in order to help him in his desperation. Having come to this conclusion the happy 'Baal-Agallah' looked for a way of expressing his gratitude to the Almighty, but the poor man knew not a Hebrew word, nor could he say any prayers. He racked his simple brain for the best way of thanksgiving.

"Suddenly his face lit up. He took his whip and lashed it into the air with all his might, crying out with all his being:

" 'O, dear Father in Heaven, I love you very much! What can I do to convince you of my love for you? Let me crack my whip for you as a sign that I love you!' Saying which, the 'Baal-Agallah' cracked his whip into the air three times.

"On the eve of Yom-Kippur the Almighty up above was seated on His 'Seat of Judgment,' listening to the first prayers of the Day of Atonement.

"Rabbi Levi Yitzchak of Zelechev (the 'Berditchever') who was acting as the Counsel for Defense on behalf of his fellow-Jews, was pushing a wagon full of Jewish Mitzvoth to the Gates of Heaven, when Satan appeared and obstructed his path with piles of Jewish sins, so that Rabbi Levi Yitzchak just got stuck there. My brother Rabbi Zusia and I added our strength to help him move his wagon forward, but all in vain; even our combined efforts proved fruitless.

"Suddenly there came the sound of the cracking of a whip which rent the air, causing a blinding ray of light to appear, lighting up the whole universe, right up to the very heavens! There we saw the angels and all the Righteous seated in a circle, singing G-d's praise. On hearing the Baal-Agallah's words as he cracked his whip in ecstasy, they responded:

" 'Happy is the King who is thus praised!'

"All at once, the Angel Michael appeared, leading a horse, followed by the 'Baal-Agallah' with whip in hand.

"The Angel Michael harnessed this horse to the wagon of 'Mitzvoth,' and the 'Baal-Agallah' cracked his whip. Suddenly the wagon gave a lurch forward, flattened out the Jewish sins which had been obstructing the way, and drove it smoothly and easily right up to the 'Throne of Honor.' There the King of Kings received it most graciously and, rising from the 'Seat of Judgment,' went over and seated Himself on the 'Seat of Mercy.' A happy New Year was assured.

" 'And now dear Rabbi Uri,' concluded Rabbi Elimelech, 'you see that all this came about through your noble action! Go home, and be a leader in Israel! For you have proved your worthiness! And you shall carry with you the approval of the 'Heavenly Court!' But before you go, permit me to hold this wonderful Ethrog of yours, and praise G-d with it."

THE REWARD

(From the Midrash)

Once upon a time there lived a very charitable man. One day — it was Hoshana Rabbah — his wife gave him ten *Shekels* and asked him to go and buy something for their children. At that moment a collection was being made in the market place for a poor orphaned girl who was about to be married. When the collectors saw this charitable person they said, "Here comes a very charitable man." They addressed themselves to him saying, "Will you take a share in this worthy cause, for we want to buy a present for the poor bride?"

The good man gave them all the ten Shekels he had. Now he was ashamed to return home empty handed, and so he went to the synagogue. There he found children playing with Ethrogim, for it was *Hoshana Rabba* (the seventh day of Succoth) and there was no more need for the Ethrogim. The good man collected a sackful of Ethrogim and went out to seek his fortune. Arriving in a strange land he sat down on his sack of Ethrogim, wondering what he was going to do next. Suddenly he was approached by the king's officers who asked him what he had in that sack.

"I am a poor man and have nothing to sell," he replied. They opened his sack and found it was full of Ethrogim. "What kind of fruit is this?" the officers asked. "These are Ethrogim, a special fruit used by Jews during their festival of Succoth."

When the officers heard that, they grabbed him and his sack and carried him all the way to the palace. It was then that our good man learned what all the excitement was about: The king was very ill and he was told that only the fruit used by Jews during their festival of Succoth could cure him. A very intensive search had yielded nothing, and just when all hope seemed to be gone, this good man arrived with a sackful of Ethrogim, and thus saved the king's life. The king recovered his health and ordered the sack emptied of the Ethrogim to be filled with golden *dinars*. Our good man now returned home richly rewarded for the charity he had been giving all his life.

THE FEAR OF G-D

"The end of the matter is, when all is heard: FEAR G-D, and keep His commandments, for this is the whole (duty of) man."

(*Koheleth* 10, 13)

Is it not strange that the above mentioned advice was given by the greatest and most powerful king that ever lived — King Solomon? Never was there a more glorious and powerful king. He ruled over a great empire, the Kingdom of Israel. G-d had granted him great wisdom, when at the age of twelve he inherited the throne from his great and illustrious father, King David. All the secrets of the Creation had been revealed to him. He understood the languages of all creatures, the animals, birds, insects, and trees. He could command the Wind, and spirits and demons served him at his will. His fame spread through the length and breath of the world. The mightiest kings and rulers in the most distant corners of the earth came to offer him their respects, listen to his wisdom, and pay him tribute.

Can you imagine a more powerful human being than King Solomon?

Usually, the more power and knowledge we have, the more we are likely to become proud and conceited. Many a man has lost his head under the influence of success and power. Such a man often forgets that even he will some day have to square his accounts before his Maker, and answer for all his actions to the Supreme King of Kings.

Not so King Solomon. The most powerful of all men lived in fear, in *fear of* G-d! He is the author of the quotation above, for he is the author of *Koheleth* (Ecclesiastes).

There could be no more qualified a man to give us such advice. He reminds us very much of Moses, the humblest of all men. Moses had every reason to be proud: G-d had chosen him to lead his people out of slavery, to receive the Torah from the mouth of G-d; had made him the leader of the nation, and his brother Aaron—the High Priest. Yet, Moses was the most modest and humble of men that ever lived. We are not impressed by the modesty of a poor and insignificant man. But Moses' humbleness was certainly wonderful to behold.

Similarly, we would not be impressed by a weak and humble person preaching submission to G-d. But it is wonderful to hear a man like King Solomon say that all his power and wealth mean absolutely nothing to him, but that the only thing of importance is to *fear G-d,* and G-d alone.

How can we acquire the great virtue of Fear of G-d (*Yirath Hashem*)? By constantly thinking of G-d's great majesty and *unlimited* power, and at the same time of our own smallness and *limited* powers. We think we are great architects: we can build a wonderful bridge, or a towering skyscraper. But what is this by comparison to the Architect of the whole Universe? We think we are great engineers: we can build a machine to give light to a whole city! But what is this by comparison to G-d's creation of the sun, which gives light and warmth and energy to the whole world? We think we are great chemists: we can make some wonderful things in our chemical laboratories. But, as one great scientist once said, the construction of the grass-blade will never be equalled.

No, we are, in reality, very small and insignificant. All our powers are limited, just as our physical life on this earth is limited. But G-d knows all (omniscient), can do all (omnipotent), is everywhere (omnipresent). All that we have is His. He created the whole universe, and He created us, for a purpose. The purpose is to understand that He is our Maker and our Master, and to fear Him. To fear Him, means to serve Him; to observe His laws and commands which He gave us in the Torah. To fear Him means to try our best to be just, honest and upright, for G-d hates injustice, and He knows all that we do, say, and even think.

Fear of G-d is the very basis of our life; without it, we would be worse than the beasts in the jungle. It is the first step on our road to a decent life.

CAST THY BREAD UPON THE WATERS

One of the very wise sayings in the Book of Koheleth is:

"Cast thy bread upon the waters, for you shall find it after many days." Which means: Always be ready to do a good turn even if you don't expect a reward for it. For, some day, you will surely find your reward waiting for you.

The following story is a very good illustration of this saying, you will agree.

Bar Kappara, one of the *Tanaim* who lived at the time of Rabbi Judah Hanassi, was once walking along the seashore of Caesaria, when he noticed a shipwreck in the distance. As he stood and looked, he saw a man swimming from the wreck towards the shore. The man seemed to be making good headway and was obviously a good swimmer. But as soon as he reached land, he almost collapsed with weariness. Bar Kappara went forward and gave him a helping hand. The man staggered ashore and begged him to assist him. Bar Kappara took him home, clothed him, fed him and offered him some money so that the man went away refreshed and encouraged.

Some years later, the Jews of Caesaria found themselves in a predicament with the local authorities and decided to send a petition to the Governor. They chose Bar Kappara to go and speak on their behalf.

Bar Kappara prayed to G-d to guide him aright and help him succeed in his important mission.

When Bar Kappara reached the Governor's palace, he asked for permission to see the Governor, having come on a very urgent matter. When his request was granted, he was ushered into the presence of the Governor. To his great astonishment, Bar Kappara recognized him as the same man whom he had once saved and helped on the shores of Caesaria.

"What can I do for you, my friend?" the Governor greeted him warmly, recognizing Bar Kappara as his one-time "friend in need."

Bar Kappara earnestly begged the Governor to use his authority in helping the Jews, on whose behalf he had now come to plead.

The Governor listened carefully and patiently to the story Bar Kappara unfolded before him and then said:

"I will gladly do this favor for you, my friend, because when I was in such a desperate position you helped me to the maximum of your ability without asking for or expecting any reward. Because of your unselfishness and kindness to me, I shall now help your suffering brethren at your request."

Bar Kappara had brought a large sum of money as a gift to the Governor from his fellow-Jews. The Governor, however, gave the money back to Bar Kappara, saying:

"Take this money back as a gift from me now. For although the sum of money you gave me was not as great as this, to me it meant everything at the time of my need. You may return to your brethren and tell them that I am helping them out of gratitude to you, and take my blessing with you."

Bar Kappara joyfully hurried back with the good news to his fellow-Jews who were anxiously awaiting his return.

Great was the rejoicing among them at Bar Kappara's good tidings, and they all acknowledged how true was the saying of King Solomon:

"Cast thy bread upon the waters for you shall find it after many days."

READINGS FROM THE TORAH ON THE FIRST TWO DAYS OF SUCCOTH

Portion: LEVITICUS 22:26 — 23:44
Haphtorah: *First Day*: ZECHARIAH 14
Second Day: I KINGS 8:1-21

The same portion is read on the first two days of Succoth. It is the well-known portion taken from *Emor*, which deals with Shabbath and all the major festivals, concluding with the festival of Succoth. This section contains the commandment of the Four Kinds (Ethrog, Lulav, Myrtle and Willow Twigs), as well as the commandment to dwell in booths (*Succoth*).

The *Haphtorah* on the First Day of Succoth is the last chapter of the Book of Zechariah. It contains a prophecy about That Day, which will be a day of reckoning for the nations of the world. The whole world will be embroiled in a terrible war, and the nations will suffer dire punishment for their mistreating the Jewish people. On that day G-d will reveal Himself in all His majesty, for "G-d will be One and His Name will be One." All the nations of the world will recognize the supreme sovereignty of G-d, and they will make pilgrimages to Jerusalem to worship Him. The highlight of the Haphtorah lies in the passages referring to the Festival of Succoth, such as: "And it shall come to pass that every one that is left of the nations which came against Jerusalem, shall go up from year to year to worship the King, the Lord of Hosts, and keep the Feast of Tabernacles." Thus, Succoth, the symbol of G-d's protection over Israel, will be especially recognized by the surviving nations of the world, and they will be rewarded for it.

The *Haphtorah* on the Second Day of Succoth takes us back to the days of young King Solomon, who succeeded his father David to the throne at the age of twelve years. In the fourth year of his reign he undertook the construction of the Beth Hamikdosh, which was completed after seven years. In the month of Tishrei the Beth-Hamikdosh was dedicated amid spectacular festivities, which lasted for fourteen days, including the Feast of Tabernacles. It is of this dedication that the Haphtorah speaks. The priests carried the Holy Ark from the City of David to the Beth-Hamikdosh. When they approached the Holy of Holies, the doors locked so that no one could enter. Solomon prayed to G-d; but it was only when he invoked G-d in the name of the great virtues of his father David, that the doors opened and the Ark could be brought into the inner Sanctuary. The young king then gratefully offered a moving prayer, the first part of which is included in the Haphtorah.

ON CHOL-HAMOED

Portion: NUMBERS 29:17-34

Four persons are called up to the reading of the Torah on each day of Chol-Hamoed Succoth, including Hoshana-Rabba. (On Shabbath-Chol-Hamoed Succoth, seven persons are called up, and an eighth for Maftir. *See below*). A short portion is read on the sacrifices which were offered in the Beth Hamikdosh on each of the remaining six days of Succoth. Included in the sacrifices were a number of bullocks each day, adding up to seventy in all during the Festival of Succoth. Our Sages say that these were offered in behalf of the seventy nations of the world.

When one of the days of Chol-Hamoed occurs on Shabbath, the reading on this day is in Exodus 33:12—34:26. This portion is always read on Shabbath-Chol-Hamoed, both of Pesach and Succoth. It is the well known portion in which we read how Moses asked G-d to reveal unto him a deeper understanding of the Divine Being. It contains the "Thirteen Attributes" of G-d. The special connection with Succoth (as with Pesach) lies in the verses which refer to the Three Pilgrim Festivals — Pesach, Shovuoth and Succoth.

A concluding portion (*Maftir*) is read on Shabbath-Chol-Hamoed in a second scroll of the Torah. This portion is taken from *Numbers* 29:17-34 (mentioned above), pertaining to the sacrifices of the particular day of Succoth it happens to be.

The *Haphtorah* on Shabbath-Chol-Hamoed is taken from *Ezekiel** 38, which contains a prophecy of the terrible war of Gog and Magog. This will be the last war ever to be fought, but it will engulf the whole world. Then will come a new era of peace, when G-d will be recognized by all the nations of the world. The prophecy, as you see, is similar to that of *Zechariah* 14, read on the first day of Succoth.

---

* About the Prophet Ezekiel, see COMPLETE STORY OF SHOVUOTH, by the author, p. 53 ff.

SUCCOTH
IN FAR-AWAY JEWISH COMMUNITIES

Among the Caucasian Jews

In the mountain region of the Caucasus, which is now part of the Soviet Union, Jews have dwelt since very ancient times. There is, in fact, a tradition among the native Jews that they are descendants of the Ten Tribes, and that their ancestors came to live there after the Kingdom of the Ten Tribes was destroyed by Shalmaneser, king of Assyria. There is also a small number of European Jews who came to live there within the last one hundred years. Among them were some Lubavitcher Chassidim who were sent there by their Rabbi to open Yeshivoth and Talmud Torahs. Thus, there was a Lubavitcher Yeshivah in the town of Kutais. In that city, as well as in the city of Tiflis, most of the Jews live. Their number is about 25,000. They speak an old dialect of Georgian; they are engaged in trade and crafts, and generally look like the non-Jewish population.

On the day before Succoth, non-Jewish farmers bring into town bundles of newly-cut green branches of needle-trees (fir and pine), which they carry on donkeys, to sell to the Jews as *Sechach* (covering for the Succah).

The Caucasian Jews build simple, small Succoth, out of four poles which they stick into the ground, with the walls also made of branches. Some make their Succoth in their yards; others—on the roof. The Succah is small, just about large enough for two or three men, the male members of the family, to get in and have their meals there. They do not decorate the Succah. Their Rabbi spends the whole week in the Succah, also sleeping in it, unless heavy rain compels him to go back to the house to sleep.

The Jews are too poor to be able to afford a Lulav and Ethrog for each family. So they have a "communal" Lulav for each synagogue. It is usually brought in from near-by Persia. The Ethrog is brought into the synagogue with great respect and love. It is placed on a shiny brass tray, and every one in turn takes the Lulav and Ethrog and kisses it lovingly, then makes the blessing, waves it, kisses it again and puts it down for the next fellow-Jew to do the same. Before long the Ethrog can hardly be recognized from so much handling and kissing.

On the night of Shemini Atzereth they make a great feast, and spend most of the night rejoicing, until the time arrives to hold the morning service. The women, too, make their own parties and celebrate the happy festival in their own way.

In Daghestan

The Jews of Daghestan are known as the "Mountain Jews." They live in the mountains of the Republic of Daghestan, which belongs to the same Caucasian region. Like their other Caucasian Jewish brethren, they have lived here from most ancient times, and they, too, believe they are descendants of the Ten Tribes. They speak a Jewish dialect of Persian. They are tall, strong and picturesque, and engage in farming, cattle raising and tanning (leather-making). In olden times they lived in separate villages of their own. Now they mix more with the non-Jewish population, but they cling to their Jewish faith and are proud to be Jews.

The Jews of Daghestan love to make beautiful Succoth, which they decorate with fine handsome rugs and carpets, at which they are experts. The Ethrogim and Lulavim are brought in from Persia, or the southern part of Russia. After prayer they greet each other joyfully and invite each other to their Succoth for refreshments.

Thus each day of Succoth is a happy day, and a good time is had by all.

On the night of Hoshana Rabba they get together in the synagogue, light candles, and the learned among them read for them the Book of Devarim, and they recite the whole Book of Psalms. At dawn they hold their morning service, recite Hoshanas and go with *Hakafoth* seven times, much in the same way as we do.

On the night of Shemini Atzereth they also have *Hakafoth* (as in most Russian communities). The women watch from the gallery, their faces hidden behind veils and kerchieves, while the boys congregate in the center of the synagogue and kiss the scrolls of the Torah. All the men and boys dance with the Torah joyfully, and recite prayers and hymns in strange melodies and tunes.

Among the Kurdish Jews

The Kurdistan country and mountains belong partly to Persia and Iraq and partly to Turkey. Here, too, Jews have lived from very ancient times, and they believe that their ancestors belonged to the exiled Ten Tribes. They number about 15,000 and engage in farming and cattle raising. Some Kurdish Jews have emigrated to the Holy Land, where they have communities of their own, and have preserved their customs, language and dress.

The Kurdish Jews are tall and muscular. They look very much like the Muslims, for they dress in the same manner. They wear heavy turbans on their heads, broad pants, with a wide belt, or girdle around their shirts, which have long sleeves and are worn over their pants. The women, too, wear roomy blouses with heavy belts, and balloon trousers. Their heads are covered with turbans, with thick black braids falling over their shoulders. The Kurdish Jews, both men and women, look very impressive in their festive dress, especially on the Sabbaths and festivals.

They pray in simple synagogues, sitting on rugs. Before entering the synagogue they take off their footwear. In the Succah, too, they sit on rugs, as at home.

Among them, as among the Caucasian Jews, there are two types: the Jews who live in the valleys, and the Jews who live in the mountains. The "Mountain Jews" are darker in skin, and have black hair. They grow beards which they never cut or trim, so that many of them look fierce in their garb with their daggers at their sides.

Their customs are similar to those of the Babylonian and Baghdad Jews. On the Sabbath and festivals, especially during Succoth, they make merry and rejoice very heartily.

In Aden

Aden is a sea-port on the Red Sea, belonging to Great Britain. The Jews here must have been among the earliest settlers. Some five hundred years ago, the great Rabbi Obadiah of Bertinoro[1]) wrote that there had come to Jerusalem "Jews from the land of Eden . . . The Jews there are dark brown. They are not much acquainted with the Talmud, but only with Rabbi Alfasi[2]) and Rabbi Moshe ben Maimon[3]) . . ."

Before the last World War there were seven synagogues in Aden, and the Jewish population numbered several thousand. The native Jews are chiefly reed-workers, mat-weavers, masons, jewellers, bookbinders and porters. They eat mostly vegetables, dates, and fish, and drink

---

1) See *Talks and Tales,* Nos. 77-79.

2) Also known as RIF, one of the earlier codifiers ("Rishonim"), who lived about 4773-4863.

3) See *Talks and Tales,* No. 14.

wine. The women wear a veil (like Mohammedan women), shirt, trousers and a wig (*sheitel*). The men wear shirt, kilt, prayer fringes, waistcoat and a long loose upper garment with a girdle around the waist.

When Succoth comes, the Jewish quarter of Aden appears like one green garden. For on the crowded roof-tops there are many Succoth, covered with green *Sechach.* The Jews of Aden sleep in their Succoth, for in any case many Jews sleep on the roof because it is cooler there. Many Succoth are beautifully decorated. Multi-colored cloths are hung on the walls, and from the Succah roof hang apples, pomegranates and Ethrogim, filling the air with a pleasant fragrance. The Jews of Aden love to sit in their Succoth. The meals last a long time, and are accompanied by songs and melodies, some in Hebrew, some in Arabic, and at night, all the Succoth are ablaze with light and color, shining through beautiful glass lamps, imported from India.

SHEMINI ATZERETH and SIMCHATH TORAH

SHEMINI ATZERETH AND SIMCHATH TORAH

SHEMINI ATZERETH

IN connection with the festival of Shemini Atzereth (the Eighth Day of Assembly) our sages tell us a fine parable: A king once arranged a great feast and invited his dear princes and princesses to his palace. Having spent several happy days together, the guests prepared to take leave. But the king said to them: "Pray, stay one more day with me, it's hard for me to part with you!"

So it is with us, our Sages conclude the parable. We have spent many happy days in G-d's house—in the synagogue. Some of the worshippers are unfortunately *rare* visitors. G-d wants to see us an extra day in shul, and so He gave us an extra festival—Shemini Atzereth.

In some congregations it is customary to have "Hakafoth" on the night of Shemini Atzereth, just like on the following night of Simchath Torah (see further).

We still eat our meals in the Succah on Shemini Atzereth, though without the blessing "to dwell in the Succah" (*Leishev baSuccah*).

The reading of the Torah during the morning service of Shemini Atzereth is the portion of "Asser Te'asser," dealing with the commandment to give tithes. Succoth is the Festival of Ingathering (*Chag Haasif*), when the harvest was gathered in from the fields. It was then the time to take off "tithe" in accordance with the commandment of the Torah and to give it to the Levites and the poor.

The "Musaph" service is marked by the special prayer for rain (*Geshem*).

Simchath Torah

At last comes the most joyous day of all--the day of Simchath Torah—rejoicing with the Torah.

After the evening prayer and Kiddush in the synagogue, the "Hakafoth" are performed by the reciting of "Atto horeiso," and the taking out of all the scrolls of the Torah from the ark, which are then carried around the Bimah in seven circuits (Hakafoth). Every one receives the honor of carrying the Torah. In between the Hakafoth, singing and dancing with the Torah is the order of the day. The little boys and girls also join in the celebration and rejoicing, and accompany the procession around the Bimah carrying their Simchath-Torah-banners with a burning candle at the top. Some of these banners are very elaborate, with miniature arks that open and close, and illustrated with pictures of Moses and Aaron and David, all rejoicing with the Torah.

The "Hakafoth" are repeated again during the morning service, with the same degree of rejoicing. After the Hakafoth three scrolls are taken from the ark for reading. In the first, the last portion of the Torah — "Vezoth Haberacha" — is read and re-read many times until every one has been called up to the Torah. Then boys who are not yet Bar-Mitzvah are called up jointly with a distinguished member of the shul ("Im kol hanearim"—with all the boys). Thereupon the blessing "Hamalach hagoel" (the angel who redeems) with which Jacob blessed Joseph's children, is said on behalf of the boys.

For the concluding portion a distinguished member is called up, and he is called "Bridegroom of the Torah." Another distinguished member is called up for the first portion of Bereishith which is read in the second Torah scroll. He is called "Bridegroom of Bereishith." Finally the Maftir is called up and the portion is read in the third scroll of the Torah, the Haftorah itself being taken from the first chapter of Joshua, Moses' successor.

Thus, the reading of the Torah goes on portion by portion throughout the year, throughout the ages, in everlasting cycles. The Torah is concluded on Simchath Torah, but it is also immediately started again from the beginning. This shows that there is no end to the Torah and that it must be read and studied constantly, over and over again. For the Torah, like G-d Himself who gave it to us, is everlasting. By observing it, our people Israel forms the third link in the eternal union between G-d, the Torah and Israel.

RAIN AND DEW

Geshem and Tal

On the Festival of Shemini Atzereth, the Musaph service begins with a special prayer for Rain ("Geshem"). From that time, and throughout the winter months, until the first day of Passover, we say in the Amidah (in the second blessing, called *Gevuroth* — mighty acts, the words, "Mashiv haruach umorid hageshem," — Who causes the wind to blow and the rain to come down. On the first day of Passover a similar prayer is recited for Dew ("Tal"), and from the first day of Passover, throughout the summer months, the words *Mashiv haruach,* etc., are omitted, and in some congregations supplanted by the words "Morid hatal," — Who causes the dew to come down.

The Prayer for *Geshem* on Shemini Atzereth (as the Prayer for *Tal* on Passover) is an impressive one. The

Baal-Tefillah or *Chazan* puts on a white *Kittel,* and recites the prayer in a solemn tune reminiscent of the Solemn Days.

The reason for these special prayers is understandable enough. The winter months in the Holy Land are the Rain Season, and the entire life of the country depends on rain. If the rains come down in their due season and in sufficient quantity, the rich soil will produce abundant crops and fruits; if not, the country is doomed to famine and starvation.

During the summer months there is no rain; it's the dry season. During these rainless months, the earth would have been completely parched, the top soil would have turned into dust and would have been blown away by the wind; the land would have turned into barren desert — were it not for the dew which settles on the cool soil during the hours of the night, drenching the ground with the soft moisture which we know as dew, and which sparkles in the early rays of the sun like pearls.

Thus, the rain in the winter, and the dew in the summer, are vitally needed to sustain life. And since we Jews recognize that it is G-d, the Master of the world, who is the Master over the wind and clouds, who makes it rain whenever and wherever He desires, we turn to G-d with our prayers for rain and dew in their proper seasons: *Geshem* on Shemini Atzereth, at the beginning of the winter season; *Tal* on the spring festival of Passover, at the beginning of the summer season.

The Prayer for Rain

The Prayer for Rain consists essentially of two beautiful and moving prayer-poems, composed by the famous *Paytan,* Rabbi Elazar ha-Kallir, who lived about 1300 years ago.

The first of these begins with the word *Af-Bri*, which is the name of the angel of rain:

Af-Bri is the title of the prince of rain,
Who gathers the clouds and makes them drain,
Water to adorn with verdure each dale,
Be it not held back by debts left stale;
O shield the faithful who pray for rain . . .
May He send rain from the heavenly towers,
To soften the earth with its crystal showers,
Thou hast named water the symbol of Thy might,
All that breathe life in its drops to delight,
O revive those who praise Thy powers of rain.

The second part of the Prayer for Rain consists of a poem beginning with the words *Zechor-Av*, Remember our father Abraham. It is an alphabetical acrostic, each line beginning with a letter of the Hebrew alphabet (excluding the word "Remember" at the beginning of each stanza), and finishing with the word "Mayim"—Water. It refers to the good deeds of our ancestors Abraham, Isaac, Jacob, Moses and Aaron, and lastly the twelve tribes, and the miracles that were shown to them in connection with water. In their merits, and for their sakes, we pray to G-d for rain:

Our G-d and G-d of our fathers,
Remember our father Abraham who was drawn after Thee like water,
Whom Thou didst bless like a tree planted near streams of water,
Thou didst shield him, Thou didst save him from fire and water,
Thou didst try him when he sowed by all streams of water.[1]

Congregation: *For his sake, do not refuse water.*

Remember Isaac whose birth was foretold over a little water;[2]
Thou didst tell his father to offer his blood like water;[3]
He too was heedful in pouring out his heart like water;
Digging in the ground he discovered wells of water.[4]

Congregation: *For his righteousness' sake, grant abundant water.*

Remember Jacob who, staff in hand, crossed the Jordan's water;[5]
His heart attuned to Thee, he rolled the stone off the well of water;[6]
When he wrestled with the angel of fire and water,[7]
Thou didst promise to be with him through fire and water.

Congregation: *For his sake, do not refuse water.*

Remember Moses in an ark of reeds drawn out of the water;[8]
They said: He drew water and provided the flock with water;
And when Thy chosen people thirsted for water,
He struck the rock and there gushed out water.[10]

Congregation: *For his righteousness' sake, grant abundant water.*

Remember the High Priest who bathed five times in water;[11]
He bent and washed his hands with sanctified water;[12]
He read from the Scriptures[13] *and sprinkled purifying water;*
He kept a distance[14] *from a people turbulent as water.*

Congregation: *For his sake, do not refuse water.*

Remember the twelve tribes Thou didst bring across the water;[15]
Thou didst sweeten for them the bitterness of water;[16]
For Thy sake their descendants spilt their blood like water;
Turn to us, for our life is encircled by foes like water.

Congregation: *For their righteousness' sake, grant abundant water.*

Reader: *For Thou art G-d, who causest the wind to blow and the rain to fall.*

Cong. and Reader:	Congregation:
For a blessing,[17] *and not for a curse*	*Amen.*
For life, and not for death	*Amen.*
For plenty, and not for scarcity	*Amen.*

Explanations

1. G-d tried Abraham with ten trials, among them was the commandment to leave his birthplace and go to the land of Canaan. Here Abraham sowed, but did not reap, for there was a famine in the land. This was yet another trial, but Abraham's heart was perfect with G-d, and he remained faithful through all his trials.

2. When the three angels visited Abraham, after his circumcision (Gen. 18), Abraham offered them "a little water" (Gen. 18:4). One of the angels told him that a son would be born to him.

3. This refers to the *Akedah,* the binding of Isaac (Gen. 22).

4. Gen. 26: 18-22.

5. Gen. 32:11. When Jacob fled from Esau, he had nothing but his wanderer's staff.

6. Gen. 20:10.

7. Gen. 32:25.

8. Exodus 2:3,10.

9. The daughters of Jethro (Exodus 2:17,19).

10. Exodus 17:6.

11. On the day of Yom Kippur, the High Priest immersed himself five times, when he changed his clothes from gold to white (linen) alternatively, for the special services he had to perform in the Beth-Hamikdosh.

12. The High Priest had to sanctify both his hands and his feet with water.

13. Yoma, ch. 1, Mishnah 6.

14. Yoma ch. 1, Mishnah 1.

15. This, of course, refers to the crossing of the Red Sea.

16. Exodus 15:23-25.

17. Rain is a blessing, but it can also be a curse sometimes, G-d forbid, if it comes at the wrong time, or brings floods, destruction, and loss of life. Therefore, we conclude the prayer for rain by praying that it bring blessings, life and plenty.

GIVE AND GAIN

The Torah commands the Jewish farmer to give away one tenth of his produce to the Levites and needy. This tenth part is called "Maasser" (tithe). On Shemini Atzereth we read a famous portion in the Torah, beginning with the words "Asser t'asser," meaning, *Thou shalt surely give tithe.*

The reason this portion is read on Shemini Atzereth, will be discovered, if we remember that Succoth is the *Festival of Ingathering* and Shemini Atzereth is the eighth day of Succoth (although it is really a separate festival). In other words, this is the time when all the produce of the land has been gathered in. It was, therefore, the time of giving away what was due to the Priests and Levites and other landless and needy people.

Our Sages see in the words *Asser t'asser* an indication of a promise of riches to him who faithfully observes the law of Maasser. For the Hebrew words *asser* (to give a tenth part) and *osher* (riches) are derived from the same root. And so their saying became famous: *Asser, bishvil shetisasher,* meaning, *Give away a tenth that you may become rich.*

The Talmud contains many stories of how people who observed the law of Maasser were amply rewarded. We will tell you one story here.

Once upon a time there lived in ancient Israel a farmer whose land produced a thousand bushels of wheat, year after year. Being a pious Jew who observed the Mitzvoth of the Torah, his first act after harvesting was to set apart a full tenth of the produce as a Maasser. In his case, it was one hundred bushels of wheat, which was quite a substantial fortune. But the farmer cheerfully gave it away to the servants of G-d in the Beth Hamikdosh and to the needy. The remaining nine hundred bushels were more than enough to take care of all his needs, with a tidy sum of money in savings. The man was getting more prosperous every year.

The time came to leave this earthly world, and the pious and wise farmer called his only son to his bedside:

"My dear son," said the dying man, "G-d is calling me, and I am happy to go, for I lived a good life, in accordance with the commandments of our holy Torah. Whatever I possess will now be yours, to do as you please. One thing I want to advise you. Our land produces one thousand bushels a year; never fail to give Maasser, and it will not disappoint you."

The old man was gone, and his son now became the owner of the farm. When harvest time came, the land produced one thousand bushels of wheat, as ever before. The son set apart one hundred bushels for Maasser, as his father had done.

Twelve moons passed, and once again it was time to

give Maasser. Now, the possession of wealth had had a bad influence on the young man. He thought that it was a shame to give away such a fortune, and he decided to give only ninety bushels, instead of the full one hundred.

The following year, however, the land produced not one thousand bushels but nine hundred.

Seeing his income decreased, the young farmer decided to make up some of the loss by reducing his Maasser. Instead of giving away ninety bushels, he gave away only eighty.

He waited for the next year's harvest quite impatiently. To his consternation, the land produced only eight hundred bushels!

Do you think the young man realized that he was playing a dangerous game? Indeed, no. He became stubborn, and kept on reducing the quantity of his Maasser. At last a point was reached when his land produced only one hundred bushels, just as much as the Maasser which was given away in the good old days when his father lived.

The foolish young man was filled with anger and sorrow. He invited his friends and relatives to his house, to comfort him in his misfortune.

At the appointed time, the invited guests appeared. But instead of giving him a sympathetic look and trying to comfort him, they looked as though they had come to celebrate.

The young man nearly lost his temper. "Have you come to insult me, and mock me in my misfortune?" he cried with grief.

"Far be it from us," replied the guests cheerfully. "We have come to celebrate with you the transfer of your land from your hands into the hands of G-d. You see, until now you had been the owner of the fields, and you had given a tenth part of its produce to G-d's charges. Now, however, G-d owns the land, and you are His charge, receiving a tenth part of what the land can produce. You have thus joined the ranks of the Levites, and we have come to congratulate you. . . ."

The young man well understood the lesson which his friends taught him. He decided to change his evil ways. How right were the Sages when they said, "*Asser, bishvil shetishasher.*"

TZEDAKAH (CHARITY)

On the High Holidays, when we appear before G-d for judgment of our deeds, we are reminded that whatever we might deserve for our record, we can always avoid an evil fate by *Teshuvah, Tefilah* and *Tzedakah* — repentance, prayer and charity.

Repentance means sincerely regretting any misdeeds in the past and a resolution to do only good deeds in the future.

Prayer is the means of communing with G-d; our three daily prayers, morning, afternoon and evening, are in the Siddur.

We shall now speak at some length about *Tzedakah.*

Our Sages often speak of Tzedakah as a great Mitzvah which can even save from certain death. The reason why Tzedakah enjoys such great merit is the fact that it represents a "total" effort on the part of the giver. What we mean by this is that, whereas any other Mitzvah is fulfilled by a certain *part* of the body, for instance, Tefillin is put on the arm and head, study of the Torah requires mental concentration, and so on, Tzedakah is a contribution made by the *whole* body, for it takes the whole of one's being, physical and mental, to do a job and earn money. Any part of it, given to charity, is a part of that *total* effort. In addition, charity given to a poor man often saves his life, or, at least, gives him life for a certain time. That is why Tzedakah has that "life-saving" quality.

There are many stories in the Talmud telling how Tzedakah saved the life of the giver from certain death. Here is one of them:

In the market place of a certain town in ancient Israel sat a famous astrologer who could foretell the fate of people by his knowledge of the stars. At that very moment two students of Rabbi Chanina passed by, carrying axes. They were obviously going to the woods to chop some firewood for the Beth Hamidrash.

The astrologer saw them from a distance and said to the people around him: "See those two young men walking yonder and chatting so amiably and happily? They do not know that death is lurking for them in the forest. Watch, and you will see that they will not return alive."

The two students continued their way, quite unaware that they were the subject of conversation, and of a rather dreadful one at that.

On the outskirts of the town they were met by a beggar who begged them for food.

"Have mercy on me, noble men. I am starving; give me some food, please," begged the man.

Although the students had but a piece of bread each to still their hunger for the rest of the day, they readily shared their bread with the beggar and went on their way, continuing to discuss the teachings they had that day learned from their great master.

Shortly before sunset the two students were ready to return to town, having gathered all the wood they could carry.

They walked back as merrily as ever, carrying on a

lively discussion on their way. As they neared the market place where the astrologer was still entertaining the crowd, there was quite a stir among the people around the astrologer. Some of them began to mock the stargazer, "Hey, you all-knowing prophet! There are two corpses walking yonder! Your stars let you down. The two students seem quite hale and hearty, and very much alive indeed!"

The astrologer, who had not failed to notice the two young men, was genuinely amazed, but not speechless.

"I still maintain," he said, "that the fate of every person is clearly written in the stars, if you can read their language. I tell you, these two young scholars were definitely destined to die this very day through a terrible accident, but somehow they succeeded to cheat death. We'll soon find out."

Saying this, the astrologer raised his voice, calling the two students to him. When they came up to him, he said to them, "Do you mind if I see what you have in your bundles?"

The two students readily threw down the two bundles on the ground. The astrologer began to rummage among the firewood, and presently his face lit up. He found a dead snake, cut in two, first in one bundle, then in the other.

"You see," said the astrologer triumphantly to the people around him, "you see how close they were to death. These snakes are the deadliest; their sting means certain death. But let us see what happened," he went on, turning to the students who stood there quite pale with fright at the thought of their miraculous escape. The astrologer asked them to recount all that happened to them that day.

The students had little to tell, except the incident with the beggar whom they had fed on their way to the woods.

"Do you understand, my friends?" exclaimed the astrologer. "The stars were not wrong. But the G-d of the Jews can be appeased by a crust of bread given to a poor man! That act of charity, small though it may seem, saved their lives from certain and painful death!"

This is but one of many stories which our Sages tell us about the greatness of Tzedakah.

If we translate Tzedakah to mean "charity," it is only because it is hard to find an English word that could really give the true meaning of Tzedakah. This is because the Jewish view on Tzedakah is quite different from that of "charity." People usually think that when they give a donation to a poor man or to a needy institution, they give something that is entirely theirs and, therefore, do an act of kindness thereby, for which they deserve thanks and gratitude. But the word *Tzedakah* in Hebrew really means *an act of justice.* To give Tzedakah is something which we are required to do not out of the kindness of our heart but out of a sense of duty and obligation, like paying a debt.

We Jews believe in G-d—not only that G-d created the world, but also that He conducts and guides the world, and the individual destinies of men, animals, and even inanimate (not living) things (like flowers, leaves, even a particle of sand on the beach). Everything and anything we have is given to us by G-d, for everything is His. When we give something to the poor and needy, we do not give of our own, but of G-d's; we are G-d's "trustees" or "agents." Therefore, it is not an act of grace on our part, which we do out of the goodness of our heart, but it is a duty and a debt. It is the same as if someone gave us a sum of money and said to us, "Take so much for yourself, and the rest give to the poor."

Nevertheless, because it is something of a test to part with money, and we are tempted to part with as little as possible, G-d rewards us very generously for giving Tzedakah "on His account," so that Tzedakah is a very good investment, whichever way you look at it.

Now, we have a little more to say about this great Mitzvah. The question is, how much Tzedakah must we give?

You see, every Mitzvah has certain regulations as to size and quantity. For example, Tzitzith must have four threads doubled over to make eight on each of the four corners, and the garment itself has to be of a certain size; so has Tefillin to be of a certain size; the Succah has its measurements; and so on. Tzedakah, too, has its regulations. According to our Law, we are expected to give at least one tenth of our income for Tzedakah. If we feel that we want to give more, we should give up to twice this amount, that is, up to a fifth of our income. In percentages it comes out between 10 and 20 per cent. (It is interesting to note, that according to American law, a person may take off from income tax up to 15 per cent of his income which is given to charity).

A wise sage,* however, said that if we want to give more than a fifth of our income for Tzedakah, we can safely "break" this law and be much the better for it. If a person can truthfully say that he has never broken any law, and leads his life strictly according to the Shulchan-Aruch (the Code of Jewish law), he can also follow strictly the rule of Tzedakah in the amount of 10 to 20 per cent of his income. But who can honestly say that? Surely, very few. It is therefore advisable for most people to overlook the limitation of 20 per cent, and give *more*. Certainly, giving more Tzedakah than the limited amount will stand one in good stead, especially when one wants to make amends for any wrong he may have committed. Be-

* Rabbi Schneuer Zalman of Liady; See footnote on p. 92.

sides, says this sage, when we pray to G-d, we do not ask Him to give us things in strict measure; we pray for His kindness and mercy which is endless and without measure. We pray to G-d to be kind and generous to us, even if we do not deserve it. Anyway, G-d does not *owe* us anything, but gives us generously all the time. So the least we can do is to act in the same way towards others who need our help.

It is especially important to remember this during the period of the Ten Days of Repentance, the Days of Judgment of Rosh-Hashanah and Yom-Kippur in particular, when our good deeds and failures are placed on the scale of justice. If Divine judgment were passed on the strict record, who could be sure of the verdict? We do not want to take such a chance. We rather pray to G-d to put away the scales and measures, and give us life and good health and all good things without measure. It would therefore be well for us to do likewise—forget the measure of Tzedakah, and give more than the law requires of us.

Now, as to the manner of giving Tzedakah. No matter what our reason may be, it is always good to give Tzedakah, for after all the poor have to be fed and clothed, and the institutions of the Torah have to be supported. So even if one gives Tzedakah because he wants to be thought of well in his community, or because he wants to be rich, or because there is sickness in the family, or because he just cannot bear the sight of a poor man—it is still a Mitzvah. The highest form of Tzedakah, however, is when one gives it because G-d commanded us to give Tzedakah, without having any thought of personal gain. That is why the highest form of Tzedakah is *Tzedakah bseiter* — anonymous contribution, where the one who benefits from it does not know the identity of the giver, and does not even know whom he is to thank for it, except G-d.

But it is not only the rich who are expected to give

Tzedakah. The law applies to every one, rich or poor. Even a beggar who lives on Tzedakah must give Tzedakah. Even a boy who receives an allowance from his father should give part of it to Tzedakah.

Then it is well to remember that Tzedakah is not necessarily a contribution of money. One can help in many other ways also: one can give of his time and effort; one can help with a word of encouragement. Above all there is also "spiritual" Tzedakah, that is Tzedakah to help spiritually. There are rich men not in money but in knowledge, and poor men not in money but in knowledge. When one who knows more Torah teaches one who knows little of it, he gives spiritual Tzedakah, which is perhaps even a greater Mitzvah than financial help. Here again there are many possibilities, especially for Yeshivah boys and girls to practise Tzedakah towards boys and girls who are "poor" in knowledge of the Torah.

While Tzedakah is so important, and can be a real life-saver, let us not make the mistake of thinking that by giving Tzedakah we have already fulfilled all our obligations and duties as Jews. Tzedakah is but one leg of the "tripod" upon which the world rests, for our Sages tell us that the world rests on three things: on the Torah, Divine worship (prayer) and *Gemiluth-Chasadim* (the practice of loving kindness, to which Tzedakah belongs). Tzedakah makes one a *good man* and *part-Jew;* to be a good full Jew, it is necessary to have also the other two foundations—to have a share in the Torah, by study and the support of Torah institutions, and to serve G-d through prayer and the fulfillment of the religious precepts.

THE SEFER TORAH

Simchath Torah means rejoicing with our Torah.

Let us see how many details we know about the "Sefer Torah" (Scroll of the Torah) which we see so often in the Synagogue, and from which portions are read just as often.

We will not consider here the contents of the Torah, or the 613 commandments which it contains. We will, in passing, say but this: *Torah* means teaching, for it teaches us our way of life, the kind of life G-d wants us to lead.

What we are interested in at the moment is to see how much we know about the external appearance of the "Sefer Torah" and the material of which it is made: Is the Torah printed or hand-written? What material is used in writing a Sefer Torah? How often is the Torah read in the synagogue? and similar details.

Since we received the Torah at Mount Sinai exactly 3268 years ago at this time of writing, it has been our light and life through the ages. Not one letter of it has been changed or altered. It has been copied many times: for the synagogue—in the form of scrolls; for the house—in the form of books, the Five Books of the Chumash.

Let us watch the whole service of "Keriath Hatorah" (reading of the Torah) from the moment the scroll is taken from the "Aron Hakodesh" (Holy Ark) until it is replaced in the Ark.

At the Morning Services of Shabbath and Yom Tov this usually takes place at about the middle of the service, between *Shacharith* (Morning Service) and *Musaph* (Additional Service).

Let us imagine it is Shabbath, and the service has reached this stage. The *Chazan* (Reader) stands by the open Ark. The appropriate prayers have been recited.

The Torah has respectfully been taken from the Ark and handed to the Reader. He recites the first verse of *Shema* and certain other verses, which the congregation repeats, and then carries the Torah towards the *Bimah*. As he passes us we bend forward and kiss the *mantle* of the Sefer Torah and get a glimpse of it at close quarters. The mantle covers the scroll completely; only the two wooden handles are seen at the top and bottom. Frequently the top of the two handles is enclosed in a special silver crown, and the Sefer Torah is further decorated with a silver plate hanging in front of it, a reminder of the *Breastplate* worn by the High Priest in the Holy Temple of old. A silver pointer is also often hung upon it, to be used by the Reader.

The mantle is made of an expensive material, with fine embroidery of symbols, such as a crown, the Ten Commandments, etc.

On the Bimah the Sefer Torah is stripped of its decorations, and of its mantle.

Under the mantle there is a girdle of silk or other fine material which holds the scroll together. This is untied, and the Sefer Torah opened.

After the Reader makes sure of the place from which the reading is to begin, that is, the beginning of the weekly portion pertaining to that particular Shabbos (or the portion which is to be read if it is Yom Tov), he rolls the scroll together again, and covers it up with its mantle. Now, the first worshipper is called up to the reading of the Torah. This is a *Cohen*. He recites the blessings. The first section is read, and then he says the blessing over it. Then the second worshipper is called up. This is the *Levi*. After him follows a third, who is neither Cohen nor Levi, but an ordinary *Yisrael*. Seven men are called up on Shabbath, and an eighth, called "Maftir" (who also reads a chapter from the Prophets).

When the reading of the weekly portion is concluded, two men are called up, one—*Hagbah*—to lift up the Torah for all the congregation to see, and the other —*Gelilah*—to roll up and tie up the Sefer Torah, and "dress" it before it is replaced in the Ark. When *Hagbah* takes place, all the congregation stand up and say: "This is the Torah which Moses put before the Children of Israel,"etc.

The scrolls of the Torah are made of parchment, that is, the skin of a kosher animal, specially treated for the purpose. Needless to say, there are no skins large enough to write the whole Torah upon a single one. Therefore several scrolls (called *Yerioth*) are sewn together, each one being a square. For thread we must not use cotton or wool or anything else, but animal tendons.

The ink used in writing the Torah is not of an ordinary kind, but a special durable one. Only black ink must be used, and no other color, not even gold, may be used.

The instrument with which the writing is done is not an ordinary pen, but a quill so sharpened as to be able to write thick and thin lines, as required.

The parchment must be ruled by a stylus, which leaves an impression on it, but no color traces. This ensures even lines.

The writing must be done in the square Hebrew characters, used traditionally in writing Sifrei Torah from days immemorial. No other kind of lettering, however artistic, may be used. Some of the letters are adorned with crowns formed of short lines. But nothing is left to the artistic tastes of the scribe, for everything must be copied strictly from the traditional way handed down to us from generation to generation, since the days of Moses.

The scribe is called in Hebrew *Sofer.* The word is derived from *Sefer*—book.

Before beginning the holy task of writing a *Sefer Torah* the Sofer prepares himself suitably. He goes to the *Mikvah* for ritual immersion, to make him pure in body as well as in mind. He must spend some time in meditation and self-searching, and must direct all his thoughts to his holy task of writing a *Sefer Torah* for G-d's sake.

Every word the *Sofer* writes must be copied from a perfect text. He must not write from memory.

The script (the writing) must be clear and simple, one letter must not touch another. It must be so simple that any schoolboy who knows how to read should be able to read it.

The writing has no *vowels* (*nekudoth*), unlike the Chumash or Siddur where reading is made easy by vowels and punctuation. In the Torah there are no commas, periods or any other punctuation. Portions are divided by blank space, and this space must in turn be measured to certain lengths according to the tradition. Because the Torah has no punctuation of any kind, it is not easily read by the untrained reader, all the more so since it has to be read according to certain notes. Every Bar-Mitzvah boy has experienced the difficulties of learning to read his portion in the Torah. Yet there are many boys who read not only a short portion, but the entire weekly Sidrah in the Torah. This is quite an accomplishment.

It would be impossible to enumerate here all the laws and regulations which must be observed in writing a *Sefer-Torah,* for they are many, and they concern chiefly the *Sofer,* and not the layman.

When the Torah is all but completed, a solemn celebration is arranged, called "*Siyyum Hatorah,*" completion of the Torah. All but a few letters are inked in, and these are completed at the "Siyyum."

It is a *Mitzvah* for every Jew to write a Sefer Torah, or have one written for him.

The scrolls are attached to wooden "bobbins," called "Etz Chaim" (Tree of Life), for the Torah is referred to as a "tree of life for them that take fast hold of it." They are specially prepared wooden rollers with flat discs, one at each end. These discs are often ornamental with little mirrors inserted in the woodwork, etc. Every *Sefer Torah* has, of course, two *Etz-Chaims.* In doing *Gelilah,* the right *Etz-Chaim* must be placed above the left one, for the right one holds the scroll upon which the beginning of the Torah (*Bereishith*) is inscribed.

The *Sefer Torah* is the holiest possession of the Jew. Jews often risk their lives to save a *Sefer Torah* in case of fire. The scroll of the Torah must not be touched with the bare hand, but with a *Tallith* or other sacred object. When it is placed on a table for reading, the table must be covered with a cloth or *Tallith.*

From the respect which is due to the *Sefer Torah* one can understand the respect that is due a *scholar* of the Torah, for he is like a *living Sefer-Torah!*

Before concluding this "talk" about the Sefer Torah, there are a few questions to be cleared up as to the number of people who are called up to the reading of the Torah on various occasions, and why are several Sifrei-Torah taken out on occasion?

We have mentioned before that on Sabbath seven men are called up, and one for "Maftir." On the Three Festivals (*Pesach, Shavuoth,* and *Succoth*) five men are called up and one for "Maftir." If the festival coincides with Sabbath, then eight men are called up in all, as on an ordinary Sabbath. On Rosh-Chodesh and the week days of the Festival (*Chol-Hamoed*) four people are called up. On *Yom-Kippur*—six, and one for "Maftir." On all other occasions—three. The following table will be helpful:

Sabbath—Seven and Maftir
Yom-Kippur (if not Sabbath)—Six and Maftir
Festivals (if not Sabbath)—Five and Maftir
Chol-Hamoed (if not Sabbath)—Four
Rosh-Chodesh (if not Sabbath)—Four
Chanukah, Purim, Fast Days, Mondays and Thursdays, and Sabbath-Minchah—Three.

There are occasions when in addition to the weekly Sidrah a special portion must be read, such as that of the *New Moon* (if it occurs on a Sabbath), or any of the Four *Parshiyoth*: *Shekalim, Zachor, Parah, Hachodesh*). In that event, not one but two Sifrei Torah are taken from the Ark, so as not to have to roll the scroll back and forth to find the second portion, keeping the congregation waiting in the meantime. For this reason we take out two scrolls on a Yom-Tov, because "Maftir" is invariably read in a different portion (*Pinehas*). There are occasions when three Sifrei Torah have to be taken out, as for example on *Sabbath-Rosh-Chodesh-Chanukah.*

It is remarkable indeed that on any given Sabbath or festival, or even Monday and Thursday, the very same portion is read in each and every congregation throughout the world! Every Jewish calendar gives the name of the weekly Sidrah, and it is so much part of the Jewish calendar, that very often instead of giving the Hebrew date (the day and month) Jews use the day and the *weekly Sidrah!*

THE GREAT TREASURE

And Moses, the servant of G-d, died.
(DEUT. 34:5)

Once upon a time there lived a very poor man. All he had was an old mare, a little cart, and a spade. With these he would go out to the hills to dig up sand. He would fill a few sandbags and cart them back to town for sale. It was hard work digging sand and hauling it to town, and the income was small. But the poor man was always cheerful, as long as he could feed his hungry children and bring something for his wife, too.

One day, as the poor man was digging away, his spade struck something hard. "That's the end of the sand," the poor man said to himself, for he thought that he had reached hard rock. Imagine his surprise, when instead of a spadeful of stone he dug up a spadeful of gold nuggets! Clearing the sand away, there was before his eyes a veritable mountain of gold! The poor man could not believe his eyes.

After recovering from his surprise, the poor man emptied his sandbags and filled them with gold, as much as he could carry, not forgetting his poor, underfed mare. "Now, my faithful mare," he said to the beast, "you will be able to retire. No more lugging heavy sandbags for you. You shall rest in comfort, and have all the oats you want. Do you know what oats are? Well, no more dry hay for you. You will be the happiest mare in the town." As he was saying this to his mare, the poor man thought of his family. Never will they be hungry again; the children will go to school, his wife will be busy taking care of the house, and he will sit and learn all day, and sing G-d's praises.

When he loaded the gold on his cart, he was afraid to move in broad daylight. People would see that he was not carrying sand; there might be some thieves and robbers. It was not safe to go now, he thought, deciding to wait till nightfall.

In the meantime there was much sorrow in the poor man's home. His wife and children were waiting for him; they were hungry and worried, for the sun had set and he had not come home yet. Now his wife was certain that something terrible had happened to him; perhaps he was buried under a heap of sand, Heaven forbid?

It was growing dark. She lit a tiny lamp and continued to wait, praying to G-d that her husband be safe.

Just then she heard the creaking sound of her husband's cart. Presently, panting heavily, the husband staggered into the house with a bag on his shoulders. He threw the bag down, which, being worn and torn, burst wide open, and golden nuggets scattered all over the floor with a clang.

The wife opened her eyes wide, gasped, gave a sigh and a groan, then collapsed on the floor. The poor woman was dead.

Later the man was asked, "Why is it that when you struck gold, and found so much of it, you did not die of the surprise and shock, while your wife did?"

The man replied, "When I struck gold, I saw a mountain of it, I knew I could not take it all. This thought saddened me, for I could not take it all with me, except the little which my old mare and I could carry. My feelings were dampened and my excitement was mixed with sadness. But when I brought a bagful of nuggets to the house, my wife did not know there was more where that came from, which would never be ours. She saw so much wealth as she had never dreamed of. To her it seemed as if the gold of the whole world was hers. The excitement was too much for her, poor thing."

* * *

When the teacher finished this story, he said, "Do you know, children, why I told you this story? I told it to you, so that you would better understand our great Master, Moses. Moshe Rabbenu was the greatest prophet that ever lived, as the Torah states in its concluding verses. He was the man who came closest to G-d, and he was the wisest and most learned. Yet, the Torah tells us that he was the most humble man that ever lived! Do you know what this means? It means that Moses really believed that he was not wise enough, not G-d-fearing enough, not worthy enough. He really believed that any man of the six hundred thousand adult Jews, whose shepherd he was, was worthier than he.

"Now, how is it possible that the greatest and wisest of all men should truly think he was not wise or worthy enough? The answer is simple.

"You see, just because Moses came so close to G-d, he knew that whatever wisdom he had was so little, compared to the Source of Wisdom. Like that lucky sand-digger who discovered a mountain of gold, and could take away with him but a little, so Moses saw the great treasures of wisdom that are with G-d, and knew that almost all of it was beyond his reach, except the little which he could learn, which was like a drop in the ocean.

"And so it is, children, with all truly wise men. They know that whatever they have learned is but little, and that there is an endless treasure of wisdom, Divine wisdom, which is beyond their reach. He is a foolish man who thinks that he knows everything, thinking that the little knowledge he has is all the knowledge in the world."

HAKAFOTH UNDER FIRE

(A Story)

The *Hakafoth* were in full swing. Round and round went the circle of dancing worshippers in the little *Shul,* chanting a snappy Simchath-Torah melody and dancing rhythmically to its tune. Circles formed and reformed as some dancers dropped out exhausted and others took their place, the dancers holding each other by the hand or shoulders. Now and again someone would strike up a new tune, and the pace would quicken with the rhythm of the new melody. Those who dropped out of the dancing circle would continue to participate by swaying to and fro, clapping their hands and urging the dancers on to renewed vigor.

I had come to watch, that's all. But I had come too close to the dancing circle. Somebody from the circle grabbed me by the arm and pulled me into the whirling mass of dancers. Somewhat bewildered at first, I soon caught up with the rhythm and excitement of the dancers. I now felt part of these lovely people who were dancing and rejoicing with G-d's greatest gift—the Torah. It was a wonderful feeling.

As the circle grew I found myself pushed more and more into the center, I turned my head to steal a glance at the man who had "roped me in." He was still resting his hand lightly on my shoulder. He seemed an elderly man, and I wondered where he got so much strength to dance and dance without end. As his eyes were closed, I did not mind studying his face a little longer without seeming rude or curious. His lips were moving, but not a sound came from them. Beads of perspiration stood out on his forehead and face, and I was astonished to see that tears were streaming down his cheeks. An inner happiness and ecstasy were written all over his noble face. I felt drawn to him, and though I was almost exhausted, I should have been ashamed to admit it, seeing the lively energy of this elderly man.

Finally, the Hakafoth were over, and the circle broke up. The dancers sat down to relax and catch their breath. I followed my dancing neighbor and sat down near him.

"It's a long time since I had such inspiring Hakafoth," he said, wiping the perspiration from his face.

"Yes, it makes you feel good," I said, trying to keep up the conversation. I felt that if the gentleman would only continue to speak, it would be worth listening to.

"*Good!*" exclaimed my neighbor. "Young man, do you know what 'good' is? Have you ever felt so gratefully happy that you wept for joy?"

"Well . . ."

"Ah! Let me tell you of those Hakafoth many years ago, and you will know what I mean. . . ."

I was never more interested in my life. My neighbor must have read my eagerness, and he did not keep me in suspense.

"It was about thirty years ago. Let me see, yes, exactly thirty years ago today, or rather to-night. Those were the terrible days after the first world war. I lived in Riga then, the capital of the newly born independent Republic of Latvia.

"That night of the Hakafoth we were sheltering in a cellar in the old city. The thud of cannon bombardment could be heard in the near distance, and the rattle of machine guns. For the German insurgents under Bermont were just across the river Dvina, and the city was resolutely defended by the nationalist forces. Things were not going well for the nationalists. They were losing ground, they were nervous, and they suspected treachery and espionage. Anybody that fell under suspicion was put to the wall and shot, without even any investigation made.

"Now imagine that night, with a heavy bombardment by the enemy across the river, the sky overcast, and the whole city in a total blackout. Suddenly, sentries see a light through a window in a top floor apartment. The light dances up and down, then disappears. 'The spy nest has been discovered at last!' the sentries decide, and they rush to the house to lay their hands on the spy. They run up the steps, and down again. We can hear their heavy boots. Finally they burst into our cellar and cry, 'Where is the dirty spy?!'

As I raised my eyebrows, as if to say, I don't get it, the old man smiled.

"You are wondering what those sentries were doing in our cellar at *Hakafoth?* Well, then I must tell you about Zalman. His second name was Michelson, but hardly anyone knew it. He was better known as Zalman the Mattress-maker. He was as poor as a church mouse, but as cheerful and carefree as a lark. It goes without saying that he was a pious man. He did not know what it meant to be sad at any time, let alone at times when rejoicing was in order. Heaven knows, he had plenty to be worried about: many mouths to feed, a marriageable daughter, an ailing wife. But G-d had blessed him with a cheerful disposition, and seemingly nothing, absolutely nothing could break his spirit.

"Well, Zalman the Mattress-maker was with us in the cellar that night. That night of all nights, when Jews are expected to rejoice with the Torah, to dance with the Torah, there we were sitting downcast, depressed, shivering in our skins every time an explosion shattered the silence.

"Zalman could not stand it any longer. 'Brothers!' he exclaimed. 'It's Simchath Torah to-night! We must rejoice!' But his words fell flat upon our ears. He looked hurt for a moment, then he suddenly remembered something. 'I see, my friends, that without a drop of *shnapps* there will be nothing doing. Well, I just remembered: I have a pint of shnapps in the cupboard at home, which I have been saving for tonight. Clean forgot! I'll be back in a jiffy.'

"We looked at him in amazement. 'Are you crazy, Zalman? You cannot climb all those steps to the sixth floor, with shrapnel flying about, and bullets, and broken glass and masonry—for a pint of shnapps! Don't be a fool, Zalman.'

"But Zalman said: 'Don't worry, brethren. We have a great and mighty G-d. I'll be right back, and then we will celebrate *Hakafoth*.' And before we could hold him back forcibly, he had disappeared, taking with him a candle. . . .

"Zalman climbed to the sixth floor, where he lived. He lit the candle and found the bottle. He was so happy, that he danced about with the candle burning in one hand, and the bottle in the other, forgetting all about the war, the bombardment, the regulations. It was in this state that he finally came back to us in the cellar.

"Now, my young friend, you understand what the sentries saw in the darkness of the night. . . .

"It was just as we prepared to celebrate *Hakafoth*, that the sentries burst in crying, 'Where is the dirty spy?!'

"We were horror-struck, and remained speechless. We knew what it meant to be accused of spying. 'Turn the spy over to us, or we will have you all shot!' the sentries shouted. 'Somebody was giving signals to the enemy a few moments ago, and the arsenal is but a block away! You dirty Jews would have us all blown up, would you? For the last time, who was giving the signals to the enemy?'

"At this moment Zalman stepped forward, bottle in

hand, and calmly said: 'Officers, it was I whom you saw with a light upstairs, but I was not signaling to the enemy. I . . ."

" 'Never mind, come along!' the soldiers said briskly, and marched poor Zalman off under heavy guard.

"If we had been depressed before, now we were truly grief-stricken. Poor Zalman! He would be put to the wall and shot immediately. No questions asked. Every time we heard a burst of machine gun or rifle fire, we thought, there goes poor Zalman. Many of us cried. We immediately pledged ourselves to support poor Zalman's widow and orphans, and to place a stone on his grave, if his body were delivered to us by the authorities.

"Time dragged on slowly. We thought the night would never end. All the time we were talking about the late Zalman and his poor bereaved family. Everybody had a good word about Zalman, how he cheered everybody up at all times, how he was the life of every *Simchah,* every wedding and happy occasion, whether he was invited or not, he was always welcome. . . .

"Suddenly we heard steps, and presently in walked—who do you think? Zalman! We couldn't believe our eyes. We thought it was a ghost. But no, the bottle in his hand looked real enough. Zalman was deathly pale, but happy and smiling, as always.

"We rushed at him and nearly floored him. Everybody tried to kiss him and embrace him. There were tears in all eyes. Some of us mumbled, Blessed be He who revives the dead. . . .

" 'Stop it! Stop!' cried Zalman. 'I love you, too, but there is no time for that now. Let's celebrate *Hakafoth!*' But we would not start with Hakafoth until he told us what happened to him, and by what strange miracle he had escaped certain death.

" 'Didn't I tell you, we have a great and mighty G-d?'

Zalman began. 'Well, when I was brought to headquarters and placed before the officer on duty, he hardly looked up at me. 'To be shot!' he called out. 'No time to investigate.'

" 'I looked at the officer for a moment, a thought flashed in my mind, and I called out: 'Styopka! What on earth are you saying?!'

" 'The officer looked up sharply, gazed at me for a moment, then burst out laughing. 'What a joke! You, Zalman, a spy! Ha, ha, ha! And with that bottle in your hand . . . Ha, ha, ha! Well, well, sit down, let's talk about old times. Do you remember when I used to come to your house to remove the candlesticks on Saturday mornings, and light a fire in the winter? I used to get a nice slice of white bread, let me see, *Challa* you called it. I was a kid then, but you treated me as though I was a grown up. I loved you, Zalman. Those were happy days in our little town, quiet and peaceful. But these are grim days . . . You are lucky that I was on duty to-night. It was not even my turn, but I was substituting for a friend. You would have been a dead duck by now. But, say, what's the idea of the bottle? Is it Purim tonight?'

" 'You ought to know better, Stepan Ivanovitsch,' says I to him. 'Purim is at the end of winter, and it's the fall now. No, it's Simchath Torah tonight.'

" 'Sure, I remember. You go round and round in a circle dancing. . . .'

" 'That's what we were going to do tonight, when we were 'slightly' interrupted. . . .'

" 'Well, go back to your dancing, and say a prayer for us, Zalman. You Jews are marvellous, risking your neck for your religion, dancing in the shadow of death....'

"That was Zalman's simple story. He got a special pass to come back to us at once, and to use at all times of curfew in the future. And then we began *Hakafoth*.

Oh, those Hakafoth! I'll never forget them. Every time I celebrate Hakafoth, I remember them; for the last thirty years!"

Then he began to hum a melody: —

"Swing your feet and raise your voice,
"With our Torah, do rejoice!"

SIMCHATH TORAH OF A CANTONIST

1.

Simchat Torah in the "Soldiers' Synagogue" of the town S. in old Russia was a wonderful sight. There was true and genuine rejoicing with the Torah in that little synagogue, where most of the members were one-time *Cantonists.*

The most impressive sight was when at the height of the rejoicing, one of the old soldiers, while dancing with a Scroll of the Torah in his arms, would pull his shirt open, disclosing deep scars on his chest and shoulders, and would sing, "Torah, Torah, I love thee." After the *Hakafoth* we, the youngsters in the little synagogue, would surround him and beg him to tell us all about those scars. Spellbound we listened to his tale though we had heard it so many times before. This is what he related:

'I was a little boy of eight when the terrible order came to my father, Rabbi Shelomo, his memory be blessed, to hand over twenty boys from our town for the Czar's army.

"There was a great outcry in our small town. To all those parents who had any boys of my age, my parents included, it meant a day of judgment. If all the children in town would have died of a plague on one day, the tragedy would not have been as great as it was now.

"In my father's house were gathered all the leading members of our community. Some of the wealthier members offered large sums to the community chest if their sons were spared. But my father would have none of it. He demanded that all children be treated alike, and that the recruiting should be done by casting lots.

"Young though I was, I realized how terrible the tragedy was, and lying in my bedroom pretending to be asleep, I heard many a raised and excited voice in the adjoining room, where the meeting was taking place.

" 'And what about your Dovidel?' I shivered when I heard my name mentioned.

" 'Of course he will be no exception,' I heard my father's grave reply.

"The meeting continued almost all night, but I had fallen asleep before it ended.

2.

"When I awoke in the morning I found my mother sitting at my bedside, her eyes red from weeping and from lack of sleep.

"She embraced me as soon as I opened my eyes, and I felt two hot tears burning on my cheek.

"No words were necessary. I knew I was to be one of those boys who would be sent away from home, perhaps never to see my parents again.

" 'Don't cry mother,' I said, "I will come back.'

" 'What I am worried about, Dovidel,' my mother said, 'is whether you will come back a Jew.'

" 'Mother, I will always be a Jew,' I said resolutely.

"The scene was repeated again as I sat on my father's knee in his little study. He spoke to me for a long time.

There were no tears in his eyes, but I knew his heart was breaking.

"Father did not live long after. About a week before the boys had to be delivered, he died.

"A few days later, two strangers came to town. They said they came to buy cattle from the surrounding farmers. Rumors spread that they were kidnappers. People whispered that they had been bribed by the wealthy families to leave their children alone and to fulfill the quota by kidnapping the boys of the poor families. My father's plan was not heeded.

"The day the kidnappers came, our town seemed to have lost all its boys. Mother hid me in the cellar.

"Then the kidnappers came to our house. I heard rude voices, a faint tussle, then a gasp and a thud, as if a lifeless body had fallen to the floor. I could not stay in my hiding place. I climbed up the steps leading to the trap-door and cried, 'Mother, are you alright? Let me out!'

"The next moment firm hands grabbed me and I was taken away. I saw my mother lying on the floor. I fought desperately, but it was to no avail. I could only cry, 'You brutes, you killed my mother.'

" 'Your mother will be alright,' they said. 'Now you be a good boy or you will be sorry.'

"We boys were led away in two wagons. We were roped together, with the end of the rope tied to the wagon.

"The whole town turned out to see us off, and my mother was there too. I will never forget that parting. An armed guard surrounded our wagons and held the people at bay. But suddenly my mother tore forward and managed to throw me a little package. 'Don't forget your Bar Mitzvah,' were her parting words.

"It was a pair of Tefillin and a little prayer book, but my Bar-Mitzvah was so far off. . . ,

3.

"Well, I will not tell you what I went through in the next three years of my 'training.' It was not a military training, but a systematic preparation for conversion, with endless beatings and tortures whenever we refused to eat with our heads uncovered, or to kiss the cross; and we *always* refused.

"During these years I came to be regarded as the 'chief' of our group. Being the son of a rabbi and having learned a great deal more than the others, they all looked up to me for guidance and encouragement. I knew that if I should show the slightest weakness, the spirit of the boys would be broken by the cruel and horrible 'training' we were getting.

"Somehow, the sergeant, who was in charge of our group, got wind of it. From that time on he concentrated all the 'heavy artillery' on little me. I was to be the example for the other boys by renouncing my faith.

"Well they did not have an easy time of it, and the deep scars that you can see will tell you that I had no easy time of it either.

"One day, after a terrific beating, I was brought before the sergeant. A priest was present and he tried to appear very friendly and concerned. A long talk followed and whenever one of them stopped to catch his breath, the other one took over. I was told of a bright future, of a brilliant career in the military academy, of the dashing uniform of a general, and the honor and power of a governor; but if I refused, I would die miserably, never seeing my mother again.

"On and on they talked, but I was hardly able to follow all they said. I was only aware of an acute pain all over my body, and an agonizing thirst.

"I asked for a drink of water.

"The sergeant filled a glass of sparkling water, and as I reached for it he held it back.

" 'Not so fast, my boy, you must first give us an answer.'

" 'Please give me the water, I will give you an answer in three days,' I said desperately.

"The sergeant and the priest exchanged glances, and then I was allowed to drink the water.

"The next three days were the worst that I had ever had. I lay on my bunk with all my body aching, but worse still was my mental agony. Could I hold out much longer? Should I give in? And then, I thought of my charges, the other boys of my group, and of my parents, and I shook my head and cried, 'No, no, no!' And so, it was—yes and no, all the time.

"Finally, came the last night before the fateful day. I was visited by the sergeant. 'You are looking fine, my boy. Won't it be a great day tomorrow?'

" 'It sure will,' I replied. He went away greatly elated, feeling quite certain that the morrow would be a day of triumph for him, a day of promotion, when the general would pat him on his back and say, 'Well done, Ivan,' and the priest would bless him with eternal life for having 'saved a soul.'

"That night I had a strange dream. I was back in my little town at the bank of our stream, where I dived in for a swim. Suddenly, I felt a terrible cramp and I was unable to swim any longer. I became frightened and gasped for breath. I wanted to shout for help but could make no sound. I was drowning . . . Then I saw a straw floating nearby, and in desperation I grabbed for it. Suddenly the straw turned into a mighty golden chain, the farther end of which was firmly and securely fastened to a tree growing on the river's brink. As I caught the end of the chain nearest to me, I saw that it consisted of many links growing bigger and bigger the further removed they were from me. Then I saw golden words engraved in the links and when I looked closer I could read, 'Abraham, Isaac, Jacob,' on the biggest and remotest three links, followed by many other names so familiar to me from the Bible. When I looked at my own link I saw my own name engraved on it, and it was securely held by my father's link.

"For a moment I felt secure and happy, but then to my great horror I saw that my link was slowly breaking apart. One more minute and it would completely break away from the chain, and I would be drowned. . . .

" 'No, no!' I cried. 'Don't break!'

"I woke up with a start and my little heart was pounding away. I lay crying the rest of the night.

4.

"The big mess-hall was filled to capacity. At the dais sat many military men and among them my own sergeant and the priest. In the hall sat many young Jewish recruits from my own group, as well as from other nearby units. An elaborate affair was planned for my 'conversion.'

"When I was led up to the dais and was ceremoniously asked to declare my willingness to become a Christian, I did not answer immediately. I turned round, deliberately gazing at my fellow-Jewish recruits, at the walls adorned with various swords and sabers, and through the window into the blue sky.

"They became impatient at the head table and prompted me again to tell them of my willingness to embrace their faith.

"Then I walked up to the wall and took down a small hatchet. Returning to the table I placed three fingers on it, carefully avoiding the middle one around which I hoped to wind the straps of Tefillin one day, and before anyone realized what I was about to do, I lifted the hatchet and brought it down with all my strength upon my fingers.

" 'There is your answer for the three days!' I said, waving my bloody hand in their faces. The next moment I fainted."

* * *

Here the old *Cantonist* paused and looked with pride at his left hand where the tips of three fingers were missing. He told us no more, but we knew that it was this very aged soldier who brought about the repeal of the Czar's cruel decree. For the story of the young boy's heroism and devotion to his faith was the talk of the whole imperial court. When Czar Nicholas heard of it, he knew that so long as there were boys like this David among his Jewish subjects, all his decrees were doomed to failure.

We looked admiringly upon the aged *Cantonist*, but hero worship was something he could not stand. He jumped up from his place and went a-dancing and singing:

"The Torah is our only choice.
"On Simchat Torah—rejoice, rejoice!"

READINGS FROM THE TORAH ON SHEMINI-ATZERETH

Portion: DEUTERONOMY 14:22 — 16:17

Haphtorah: I KINGS 8:54 — 8:66; *in some congregations to* 9:1

The reading on Shemini Atzereth is the famous portion of *Asser-t'asser,* to which we have already referred.* It begins with the laws of tithes (*Maasser* — a tenth part of the produce given away). Succoth, the Festival of Ingathering, was the time when the various tithes were given away to the Levites and to the poor. There were two tithes each year. The First Tithe had to be given to the Levites, and the Second Tithe had to be taken to Jerusalem and enjoyed there. Every third and sixth year there was a Poor Man's Tithe instead of the Second Tithe. (No tithes were due from anything that grew on the seventh ["Sabbatical"] year, which anyway did not belong to the owner, but was free to all.)

The portion also speaks of the Sabbatical Year (*Shemittah*) and the remission (forgiveness) of debts, as well as the liberation of slaves on that year.

---

* Page 180.

For *Maftir,* in the second Torah, a short portion is read from *Numbers* 29:35-39, on the sacrifices of the Eighth Day, Shemini Atzereth.

The *Haphtorah* is a continuation of the theme of the Haphtorah of the first day of Succoth. After King Solomon concluded his moving prayer and supplication, pouring out his heart to G-d in the Beth Hamikdosh just completed, he rose to his feet and blessed the people of Israel. We quote some of his concluding words, for they are truly inspiring:

> "Blessed be G-d who hath given rest unto His people Israel, according to all that He promised; there hath not failed one word of all His good promise, which He promised by the hand of Moses His servant. May G-d our G-d be with us, as He was with our fathers; let Him not leave us, nor forsake us; that He may incline our hearts unto Him, to walk in all His ways, and to keep His commandments, and His statutes, and His judgments, which He commanded our fathers.
>
> "And let these my words, wherewith I have made supplication before G-d, be nigh unto G-d our G-d day and night; that He maintain the cause of His servant, and the cause of His people Israel at all times; that all the people of the earth may know that G-d is G-d, and that there is none else.
>
> "Let your heart therefore be perfect with G-d our G-d, to walk in His statutes, and to keep His commandments as on this day."

We can well imagine how great was the rejoicing and inspiration on that eventful Succoth, when the newly built magnificent Beth Hamikdosh was dedicated. We are told in the Haphtorah that "On the eighth day he

(King Solomon) sent the people away, and they blessed the king and went to their tents joyful and glad of heart for all the goodness that G-d had done for David His servant and for Israel His people."

READINGS FROM THE TORAH ON SIMCHATH-TORAH

Portion: DEUTERONOMY 33 — *to the end of Chumash*

GENESIS 1:1 — 2:3

Haphtorah: JOSHUA 1

On Simchath-Torah, the Torah is concluded and is begun again from the beginning. Thus, on the day of Rejoicing with the Torah we complete the yearly cycle of the weekly readings of the Torah, and begin it anew.

Three scrolls are taken out on Simchath-Torah. In the first one we read the last portion of Chumash — *V'zoth haB'rachah.* The reading is divided up into two parts. The first part is read and re-read as many times as is necessary, in order to give every one, from the age of Bar-Mitzvah and up, an opportunity to be called up to the Torah. To save time, several men may be called up together. The contents of this part are clear from the opening words, "And this is the blessing wherewith Moses, the man of G-d, blessed the children of Israel before his death." Moses mentions every tribe by name and blesses each one individually, and all Israel together. The last person of this group is called up "With all the boys," that is, with all the boys under thirteen years of age. After the reading a special prayer is recited on behalf of the boys: "The angel who redeemed me from all evil, bless the lads; and let my name be named on them, and the name of my fathers Abraham and Isaac; and may they grow into a multitude in the midst of the earth." This blessing was originally bestowed by Jacob on his grandchildren Manasseh and Ephraim (*Genesis* 48:16). Needless to say, it is an exciting and inspiring moment for the boys of pre-Bar-Mitzvah age, since it is generally the only occasion during the year when they are called up to the Torah.

The second part (from 33:27 to the end of the Torah) is reserved for the "Bridegroom of the Torah" (*Chathan-Torah*), usually a distinguished and learned member of the congregation, since this reading concludes the Torah. Before he is called up, a special blessing is recited for him. This closing section of the Torah tells of the passing on of Moses at the age of one hundred and twenty years, after seeing the Promised Land from a distance, standing on the peak of Mount Nebo. The Torah tells us that Moses died "by the Mouth of G-d," and was buried by G-d in the valley below, in the land of Moab, "and no one knoweth his burial place to this day." The children of Israel wept for Moses thirty days, but they had not been left without a leader, for "Joshua the son of Nun was full of the spirit of wisdom," and he had been appointed by Moses, at G-d's command, to succeed him. In the concluding verses, the Torah tells us that there was not a prophet like Moses before or after him, "whom G-d knew face to face." For the very last verse the congregants rise to their feet, and at the conclusion exclaim: "Be strong, be strong, and let us strengthen each other!" — a determined call to continue reading, studying and following the Torah with ever growing devotion. Our Sages tell us that these last verses of the Torah, like every other word of it, were written by Moses himself, by the word of G-d, "G-d dictating, and Moses writing it down with tears in his eyes."

In the second scroll, the Torah is begun from the beginning, from Genesis. This reading is reserved for the "Bridegroom of Bereishith" (*Chathan-Bereishith*), and the honor is again accorded to a distinguished, pious gentleman. Before being called, a special blessing is recited for him, too, as in the case of the other "Bridegroom." During the reading, when the Reader reaches the verse "And it was evening, and it was morning, the first day," the entire congregation recite this verse in unison, which is then repeated by the Reader. The same procedure is followed in the case of all the other Days of Creation. The final section, including the entire portion of *Vayechulu* (which forms the first part of the Friday-night *Kiddush*) is likewise recited by the entire congregation and repeated by the Reader.

In the third scroll the portion of *Maftir* is read, which is the same that was read on the day before (Shemini Atzereth).

The *Haphtorah* is taken from the first chapter of *Joshua*. The connection is obvious. Joshua was the successor of Moses, and the Book of Joshua, the first of the collection of the Books of the Prophets, is the continuation of the Torah. Thus the Tradition was handed down from Moses to Joshua, and from Joshua to the Elders, and from the Elders to the Prophets, and so on, in an unbroken chain, to this very day.

The last Shabbath of the month of Tishrei is called *Shabbath-Bereishith,* because we read on it this portion in its entirety. Thus, at the end of all the festivals of Tishrei we come back to *Bereishith,* to the Beginning. Here is an indication that the *beginning* of all wisdom is to know that G-d is the Creator and Master of the world. Coming back to the Beginning further indicates that we never "finish," nor "graduate," as far as the Torah is concerned. Truly endless is the Torah, "longer than the earth, wider than the ocean," for it is the wisdom of G-d, the Infinite.

It is on this note that the Jew leaves the month of Tishrei and begins his daily life in the new year. Inspired and enriched by the religious experiences of every variety, with which the month of Tishrei is so rich, he can face every challenge in his daily life with courage and fortitude, in the knowledge that he is a link in the eternal chain which unites Israel with G-d, through the Torah.

ONE OF THE THREE IS RIGHT

(*Answers on p.* 222)

1. The first day of Succoth is on:
   (a) the fifteenth of Tishrei;
   (b) the eighteenth of Tishrei;
   (c) the twenty-first of Tishrei.
2. The Lulav is taken on:
   (a) every day of Succoth;
   (b) the first day of Succoth only;
   (c) every day except the Sabbath.

3. The first time the Lulav is taken:
   (a) one blessing is recited;
   (b) two blessings are recited;
   (c) three blessings are recited.
4. The "Four Kinds" are:
   (a) one Ethrog; one Lulav; two Araboth; three Hadasim;
   (b) one Ethrog; one Lulav; three Araboth; three Hadasim;
   (c) one Ethrog; one Lulav, three Araboth; three Hadasim.
5. The most important part of the Succah is:
   (a) the walls;
   (b) the roof-covering;
   (c) the decorations.
6. During the seven days of Succoth:
   (a) all meals should be eaten in the Succah;
   (b) only one meal a day;
   (c) all meals except those on Chol-Hamoed.
7. When making the blessing over the "Four Kinds":
   (a) the Lulav should be held in the right hand;
   (b) the Ethrog should be held in the right hand;
   (c) the Lulav should be pointed downwards.
8. "Hoshana" is:
   (a) a special Succoth dish;
   (b) a special prayer said on Succoth;
   (c) a special Succoth greeting.
9. On Succoth:
   (a) the whole of Hallel is said;
   (b) "half" Hallel is said;
   (c) no Hallel is said.
10. The Succah should be covered with *Sechach* so that:
   (a) the shade is more than the light;
   (b) the light is more than the shade;
   (c) the light and shade are about equal.
11. "Hoshana-Rabba" is on:
   (a) the first day of Succoth;
   (b) the third day of Succoth;
   (c) the seventh day of Succoth.

12. On Hoshana Rabba, the procession with the Lulav in the synagogue, during the prayer of Hoshana, is made:
    (a) once;
    (b) three times;
    (c) seven times.
13. "The Day of Striking Twigs" refers to:
    (a) the first day of Succoth;
    (b) the seventh day of Succoth;
    (c) the eighth day of Succoth.
14. The "twigs" refer to:
    (a) myrtle (Hadassim);
    (b) water-willows (Araboth);
    (c) branches of the palm-tree.
15. The "Arabah" used on Hoshana Rabba consists of:
    (a) three twigs;
    (b) five twigs;
    (c) seven twigs.
16. On Hoshana Rabba it is customary to eat:
    (a) kashe;
    (b) blintzes;
    (c) kreplach.

Answers on the next page

Match the Following:

1. Shemini Atzereth	a. Prayer for Rain on Shemini Atzereth
2. Asser t'asser	b. Reading of the Torah on Shemini Atzereth
3. Geshem	c. Eighth Day of Succoth
4. Hakafoth	d. Simchath Torah
5. "Bridegroom of the Torah"	e. Called up for the first portion of the Torah
6. "Bridegroom of Bereishith"	f. Called up for the last portion of the Torah
7. Joshua	g. The first Sabbath after Simchath Torah
8. Shabbath-Bereishith	h. Maftir on Simchath Torah

Answers on the next page

ANSWERS TO TEST YOUR KNOWLEDGE

Questions on pp. 138-140

A.

1-c; 2-a; 3-c; 4-a; 5-b; 6-c; 7-b; 8-b; 9-b; 10-a; 11-a; 12-c; 13-b; 14-c.

B.

15-a; 16-b; 17-a; 18-a; 19-a; 20-b.

C.

1-c; 2-g; 3-h; 4-a; 5-b; 6-d; 7-e; 8-f.

Questions on pp. 219-221

One of the three is Right:

1-a; 2-c; 3-b; 4-a; 5-b; 6-a; 7-a;
8-b; 9-a; 10-a; 11-c; 12-c; 13-b; 14-b;
15-b; 16-c.

Match the following:

1-c; 2-b; 3-a; 4-d; 5-f; 6-e; 7-h; 8-g.

EREV-ROSH-HASHANAH

1. It is customary to rise very early for "Selichoth" on the day before Rosh-Hashanah ("Zechor Brith").—No *Tachnun* is said in the morning service, and the Shofar is *not* sounded.
2. When Friday happens to be Yomtov, it is necessary for the head of the family to make an "Eiruv Tavshilin"*) in order that it be permitted to cook food on the Friday for the Shabbos following. The "Eiruv" is prepared on the day before Yom-Tov begins. As Rosh-Hashanah may occur on Thursday and Friday, it is well to to remember this law.

ROSH HASHANAH

1. From Rosh-Hashanah until after Yom Kippur we say in the Shemone-esrei the following:

   זכרנו, מי כמוך, המלך הקדוש, וכתוב, ובספר חיים, עושה השלום

   and on week-days also המלך המשפט.
2. If you forget to say זכרנו, מי כמוך, וכתוב, ובספר חיים you do not have to repeat the Shemone-esrei. However, if you forget to say המלך הקדוש you must say the Shemone-esrei over again.
3. On the first night of Rosh-Hashanah, after the evening service, we greet each other as follows:

   To a man or boy.......... לשנה טובה תכתב ותחתם
   To a woman or girl.......... לשנה טובה תכתבי ותחתמי
   To two or more men.......... לשנה טובה תכתבו ותחתמו
   To two or more women.......... לשנה טובה תכתבנה ותחתמנה
4. On Rosh-Hashanah we dip the "Motzi" (first slice of bread) in honey.
5. On the first night of Rosh-Hashanah, after the meal is begun, we dip a piece of sweet apple into honey, make the blessing בורא פרי העץ eat it and say: יהי רצון שתחדש עלינו שנה טובה ומתוקה (May it be Thy will that Thou renew unto us a good and sweet year).

*) The blessing for the "Eiruv" is found in the Prayer Book, usually before the Festival Prayers.

6. On both days of Rosh-Hashanah, after reading the Torah and during the Musaph service, the Shofar is sounded (unless Rosh-Hashanah occurs on Shabbos and Sunday when the Shofar is sounded on the second day only).
7. The blessings before the sounding of the Shofar לשמוע קול שופר and שהחיינו should be very carefully heard and אמן should be answered. (ברוך הוא וברוך שמו should not be said.) Also the Tek'oth should be carefully heard.
8. Beginning with the blessings of the Shofar until the final Tekioth of Musaph, inclusive, it is forbidden to speak.
9. On the first day of Rosh-Hashanah (but if Rosh-Hashanah is on Shabbos and Sunday—on the second day instead), after Minchah, we go to a river, lake or well, to say *Tashlich.*
10. On Rosh-Hashanah we should be careful not to speak unnecessary and unworthy words, for the entire day should be devoted to prayer, study of the Torah, and reciting of Psalms.

THE TEN DAYS OF PENITENCE

During the Ten Days of Penitence (Rosh-Hashanah through Yom Kippur), the prayer אבינו מלכנו is said in the morning and afternoon services, excepting Friday's Minchah, Shabbos and Erev-Yom-Kippur.

YOM-KIPPUR

1. On Erev-Yom-Kippur, "Kapparoth" should be observed.
2. It is a Mitzvah to eat more than usual on Erev-Yom-Kippur.
3. If an offense was committed against a fellow-man which had not been rectified yet, it must be done on Erev-Yom-Kippur without fail.
4. At the Minchah prayer of Erev-Yom-Kippur, we say על חטא at the conclusion of the Shemone-essrei.
5. The fast of Yom-Kippur begins when it is still day-light, and ends when it is definitely night.
6. Boys from the age of 13 years, and girls from the age of 12, must fast the whole of Yom-Kippur. Younger ones, and sick persons must consult a learned orthodox Rabbi.
7. From Erev-Yom-Kippur before sun-set until the end of Yom-Kippur at night-fall, it is forbidden to wash oneself; upon arising it is permitted to wash the fingers only.

8. It is forbidden to wear leather shoes on Yom-Kippur even if they are partially made of leather.
9. At the conclusion of Yom-Kippur, Habdalah is said.
10. At the conclusion of Yom-Kippur we should be joyful, in the hope that G-d has accepted our repentance and prayers, and granted us a happy New Year.
11. From the morning after Yom-Kippur, until the end of Tishrei no Tachanun is said.

SUCCOTH

1. Throughout the festival of Succoth it is forbidden to eat outside of the Succah any meal in which bread or cake the size of an egg is eaten.
2. On the first two nights of Succoth, we must eat in the Succah at least a piece of bread the size of an olive (about half an egg in size), even though we may not feel hungry, or even if it rains very hard and does not seem likely to stop soon.
3. At all other times during the festival, if it rains so hard that the food would get spoiled by the rain, we need not eat in the Succah.
4. At every meal eaten in the Succah, following the blessing המוציא (or בורא מיני מזונות) add the blessing לישב בסכה. If we remain in the Succah from one meal to the other, it is not necessary to make the blessing לישב בסכה again.
5. Women are not obliged to eat in the Succah.
6. Until after Simchath Torah, it is not permissible to use either the boards of the Succah or the "Sechach" for any other purpose.
7. Beginning with the first day of Succoth (but if it is on Shabbos, beginning with the second day) through Hoshana Rabba, we must make the blessing over the Four Kinds every day, excepting Shabbos.
8. Before saying the blessing over the Ethrog, the Lulav (to which the Hadassim and Araboth—the twigs of myrtle and willow—are bound) should be taken in the right hand, and the blessing—על נטילת לולב should be said. (When the Ethrog is taken for the first time, this blessing should be followed by the blessing of שהחיינו). Thereupon the Ethrog is taken in the left hand, while still holding the Lulav in the right hand, and the hands should be drawn close together. The "four kinds" should be waved together, and the procedure is thus concluded.
9. If one did not have an Ethrog in the morning, he can still say the blessing over the Ethrog later, as long as it is still day-time.

HOSHANA RABBA

1. The seventh day of Succoth is Hoshana Rabba. The night before, we say "Tikkun."
2. In the morning service we say all the "Hoshanas," after which we strike the floor 5 times with the "Hoshana" (a bundle of 5 twigs of willow).

SHEMINI ATZERETH AND SIMCHATH TORAH

1. The eighth day of Succoth is Shemini Atzereth and the ninth—Simchath Torah. On both Shemini Atzereth and Simchath Torah שהחיינו is said.
2. On Shemini Atzereth we must still eat in the Succah but without the blessing לישב בסכה.
3. In the Musaph of Shemini Atzereth we begin to say משיב הרוח ומוריד הגשם right through the winter, until Musaph of the first day of Pesach.
4. On Shemini Atzereth and Simchath Torah we should rejoice with the Torah.
5. On the night of Shemini Atzereth and the following night of Simchath Torah, as well as on the morning of Simchath Torah, Hakafoth are observed.
6. On Simchath Torah, every one should be called up to the reading of the Torah. Also young boys under the age of thirteen are called up to the Torah in the company of a grown-up. On Simchath Torah the Torah is concluded and is begun again from the beginning—Bereishith, showing that the Torah has really no end.

ISRU-CHAG

The day after Simchath Torah (like the day after the other major festivals) is called Isru-Chag — the day attached to the holiday, and is more than an ordinary day (it calls for more festive meals than otherwise, etc.).

A MESSAGE FROM THE LUBAVITCHER REBBE
שליט״א

ב״ה

Dear Friend:

The month of Tishrei is very colorful. Every possible atmosphere of Jewish life finds expression in this month, in which we have Solemn Days, Fast Days, and Days of Rejoicing. It is not a coincidence that the first month of the year has "samples" of every shade and color of Jewish life, for these "samples" are intended to give us an introduction to, and practical guidance for the rest of the year. By observing the special days of Tishrei in their proper spirit, we are initiated into a truly Jewish life, in accordance with the spirit of the Torah, during the whole year following.

What can we learn from the special days of Tishrei?

a. To begin with we have *Rosh-Hashanah,* the beginning of the New Year, the day when the first man just created proclaimed G-d's sovereignty over the whole Universe. When we are about to begin anything, we must always remember that G-d is the Creator of Heaven and Earth and the sole Ruler of the Universe, and that our action or venture must have Divine approval. This is further emphasized by—

b. *The Ten Days of Repentance* which remind us that since we are the servants of the King of the Universe we must keep a check on our deeds to ensure that they comply with the wishes of the Master. However, since we are only human beings, we are liable to fail on occasion. This is why G-d gives us—

c. *Yom-Kippur* to impress upon us the realization that it is never too late to turn back to the right path, provided we do it sincerely, completely repenting of, and casting away, our evil habits of the past, and solemnly undertaking to mend our ways in the future. If we make this firm resolution, G-d will forgive us, and "cleanse" us completely of our sins. Difficult though this path may appear to be,—

d. *Succoth* helps us not to despair in our days of trial, even if we find ourselves in the minority, for G-d is our protector, as He clearly showed us by the Clouds of Glory with which He surrounded us during the forty years' wandering through the desert after the Departure from Egypt. Finally, in order to know how to lead our lives so as to comply with G-d's wishes, we have,—

e. *Shemini Atzereth* and *Simchath Torah,* for in the Torah G-d has given us Divine laws of justice and righteousness and a true guide in life; by shaping our lives accordingly we are assured of true happiness, both in this world and in after life. For the Torah is a "tree of life to them that take fast hold of it, and its supporters are happy."

These, briefly, are some of the main lessons of Tishrei and there can be no doubt that by following them faithfully, the New Year will be a happy one, both spiritually and materially, and the blessing which we give each other לשנה טובה תכתב ותחתם will surely be fulfilled. That is what I wish every one of you.

RABBI MENACHEM M. SCHNEERSON

INDEX

הוצאת ספרים
קרני הוד תורה
קה"ת
ליובאוויטש